O. J.

The Story of Football's Fabulous O. J. Simpson

About the Book

The greatest runner in the history of both professional and college football—that's the record set by gracious, generous O. J. Simpson. It has not been easy for him. In this book there is the exciting story of a sickly, skinny youngster from a San Francisco ghetto who overcame obstacles to be the star of a national championship team at the University of Southern California and the winner of the coveted Heisman Trophy. Next he becomes the leader of a laughed-at last-place team in Buffalo as it begins its rise toward the top of the National Football League, winning his conference's Player of the Year award. Here the reader is taken through thrilling game after game as O. J. Simpson has played them for the USC Trojans and the Buffalo Bills, breaking records as he dodged tacklers and controversy every step of the way.

O.J.

The Story of Football's Fabulous O. J. Simpson

by Bill Libby

G. P. Putnam's Sons   New York

For Jill Fulton. And Liz Fulton.
Two lovely ladies in search of the good life they deserve.

The author wishes to thank O. J. Simpson and Chuck Barnes for all past interviews. He wishes to thank John McKay, Don Anderson, and Russ Ewald of USC and Jack Horrigan and Don Phinney of the Buffalo Bills for all help, past and present. And finally he wishes to thank Dwight Chapin, Steve Bisheff, Bud Furillo, John Hall, Allan Malamud, Bob Oates, Paul Zimmerman, Larry Felser, Charley Bailey, Harley Tinkham, Frank Deford, Edwin Shrake, Mal Florence, Dan Jenkins, John Devaney, Jim Peters, and all other writers who by having written so well about Simpson and his teams and his games have contributed so much to my knowledge of these and to this book.

Copyright © 1974 by Bill Libby
All rights reserved. Published simultaneously in
Canada by Longman Canada Limited, Toronto
SBN: GB-399-60874-5
SBN: TR-399-20384-2
Library of Congress Catalog Card Number: 73-88519
PRINTED IN THE UNITED STATES OF AMERICA
10 up

Contents

1 The Biggest Game 7
2 "Pencil-Pins" 18
3 O.J. in JC 28
4 O.J. at USC 41
5 The Schlepper 56
6 The Big Tests 64
7 Harder and Harder 78
8 Concluding a Career 92
9 The Greatest Collegian 104
10 Reaching For a Rainbow 112
11 Life-Style Of a Star 122
12 Shuffle off to Buffalo 131
13 A Rough Road 145
14 It Takes Time 157
15 Super-Pro at Last 170
Index 189

1 The Biggest Game

It was a classic contest, which O. J. Simpson calls his greatest and most thrilling game.

It was USC against UCLA, which is always a big game. No other city has within its boundaries two such large colleges that annually produce sports powerhouses. But in mid-November of 1967 there was more to the meeting than merely the usual intense rivalry. It was more than just a big game. It was the biggest game.

It was the two top contenders for the conference title, a trip to the Rose Bowl and the national crown all rolled up in one.

USC had trimmed Texas and Michigan State and thrashed Notre Dame and had been the Number One team in the national polls most of the season. UCLA had beaten Tennessee and Penn State, but been tied by tough Oregon State and so had trailed USC in the ratings. But then, as it looked ahead to its battle of the unbeatens with UCLA, USC had been upset, 3–0, by Oregon State in the rain and mud of the Northwest, and had fallen behind the Bruins, who now were Number One. And since no other team in the nation had a better record, it came down to this contest to settle the issue.

It also was a clash of coaches, USC's John McKay

and UCLA's Tommy Prothro, two of the best. Large, lumbering, intellectual Prothro had won both meetings with McKay since taking over the Bruins. Small, slick, wisecracking McKay, in his seventh season with the Trojans, didn't like these big-game losses at all, was sensitive to hints he'd been outsmarted, and hungered for revenge.

It also was, finally, a duel of individuals, USC's Simpson and UCLA's Gary Beban, who were regarded as the two top contenders for the Heisman Trophy, symbolic of the outstanding individual in college football. Beban, a senior quarterback, had passed for more than 1,000 yards. Simpson, a junior halfback, had rushed for more than 1,200 yards.

It was on many counts the biggest game of that season, if not of any season in the history of college football. For weeks, the drums had been rolling. National magazines featured stories on the stars and their teams. Newspaper columnists across the country wrote of the impending struggle, which was to be carried on national television.

In Los Angeles, newspaper sportswriters and radio and television sportscasters wrote or spoke of little else and as the fateful Saturday approached, the pressure on the young athletes grew to enormous proportions. "That morning, I felt sick," O. J. Simpson had admitted. "My guts were all twisted up. It was almost too much to take. It meant more to me than it should have. It meant everything."

He was the workhorse of his team. He carried the ball more often than any runner ever before on this level of competition—an average of twenty-six times a game. Injured a few weeks earlier, he had missed only one game when he was supposed to miss the rest of the season and now he played in a special, sponge-padded shoe to protect his sore and strained right foot.

A handsome youngster out of a black ghetto in San Francisco, he had emerged from the obscurity of two seasons in junior college play to run his way spectacularly into national prominence in this one season, which was far from finished. But now the slender but strong sprinter with dazzling moves and explosive speed limped through his final workouts and worried through the final hours before the biggest game.

He sat on the sidelines during practice, hunched over, sweat streaming down his coffee-with-cream colored skin, his uniform soiled and soggy, staring at a scraped and slightly bleeding hand, and he said, "I'm ready. I suppose I could be more ready. I could have two fine feet. But I'll forget about it if I can. I'll just play. I'll just do what I can. If I do my best, no one can complain, can they?" he asked.

Some of the students of the two schools started to converge on the cavernous Coliseum at dawn. Through the morning, as the customers in their cars began to curse the traffic jams forming in the streets of the surrounding slum area, the big bowl adjacent to the USC campus began to fill up. The big-money men and the more affluent alumni came last, moving into the best seats.

By game time more than 90,000 persons were in the ancient arena, built before the 1932 Olympics. It was a splendid southern California afternoon which confronted them, a bright hot sun slicing through the thick smog where winter arrives on tiptoe and often goes unnoticed entirely. USC's great white horse was ridden around the surrounding track. The great, big marching bands of the two schools blasted traditional music, full of football and fight. The cheerleaders, boys and girls, bounced up and down pleading for preliminary support from the stands.

The noise rose higher. And then the scarlet-and-gold uniformed Trojans and the blue-and-gold-clad Bruins streamed onto the field and a great roar exploded from the fans and confetti flew through the air and the excitement mounted to an explosive peak. The game was a gun with the trigger cocked. The scene was wild and wonderful. The drama was ready to unfold.

It could have been a bust, of course. Such games often are—full of fumbles and interceptions and other mistakes, the tension twisting the performers until they fail and the game goes dull and dead. But, as it turned out, it was not. It was all it was expected to be, and more. It was two superly coached and outstanding college teams with superstars showing off their finest form in a bitter battle.

From the kickoff, at first, it was UCLA's game. Beban paced a drive with good gains on a completion and a run, then handed off to Greg Jones, who blasted 12 yards for the first touchdown. Zeno Andrusyshyn place-kicked one of his patented low line drives through the uprights to make it, 7–0. That name was pronounced "Andrew-sish-un" and a key figure he was to be.

While Simpson was being held to 11 yards on his first ten carries, USC was held without a first down for its first five series. Meanwhile, Beban had the Bruins marching again as time was running out in the first quarter and his supporters were roaring.

On the final play of the first period, Beban threw to Jones who was open wide left past midfield, but the ball was not thrown sharply and Trojan defensive back Pat Cashman cut in front of the receiver and intercepted the throw with an open field in front of him and ran 55 yards to a touchdown as the Trojan rooters came alive. The extra point by Rikki Aldridge knotted it at 7–7.

This seemed to revive USC spirits. The Bruins battled back, but were foiled. Mark Gustafson returned the kickoff 42 yards and UCLA rolled down to the 15. However, three plays failed and on the third, Beban, who was playing with bruised ribs, got rapped in the ribs by Cashman and went writhing in agony to the sidelines. Andrusyshyn tried for a field goal from the 20, but was wide left.

USC took over and Toby Page reversed the ball to swift receiver Earl "The Pearl" McCullouch, who streaked down the sideline 52 yards before being brought down. Page then pegged to McCullouch for 13 more yards. And with the ball on the 13, he handed off to Simpson, who drove over guard through a tackle, twisted past another, and another, and another, and another, and carried a tackler over the goal line with him to an ovation.

It was only 13 yards, but veteran Georgia Tech coach Bobby Dodd later said, "It was the strongest run I ever saw made by a college boy." En route, Simpson broke six tackles. More than half the opposing team hit him and he just ripped right through their arms and drove into the end zone with the touchdown. And Aldridge place-kicked the pigskin through the uprights to make it 14–7 and confetti came streaming down on the USC side of the stands.

These Bruins were not a team to be broken easily, however. Beban, gasping for breath from his sore chest and sides, got the ball again and promptly threw it 48 yards to Dave Nuttall. Again the Bruins reached the 15 with a first down, but again the Trojans braced. Beban, who was sacked nine times by the aggressive USC defenders during the day, got banged again and again.

On fourth down, Andrusyshyn went for the field goal from the 20 again. Again he failed. This time, his usual low shot was blocked by six-foot eight-inch Bill Hayhoe, a giant introduced into the situation by McKay for the specific purpose of looming up in midline, lifting high, raising his arms, and, it was hoped, deflecting one of Andrusyshyn's low liners, which he did.

They went to intermission weary and returned ready to renew the battle. The Bruins burst out like uncaged bears. Under a rush, Beban pegged to George Farmer who broke free and ran into the end zone to complete a 53-yard scoring play. Andrusyshyn split the uprights to tie it at 14–14.

Simpson began to break free for short gains. It followed his pattern. As the others wearied and seemed to weaken, he seemed to get stronger. He kept carrying the ball and his yardage kept mounting. But he couldn't break free and the Trojans couldn't finish off a drive.

A poor punt by Aldridge gave the Bruins good field position and a perfect pass by Beban gave them a first down on the Trojan 17. But on first down, Hayhoe hurried in to blow Beban down. Two plays later, Andrusyshyn tried for the tie-breaking field goal, but there was Hayhoe looming up again and he deflected the ball again.

Into the fourth quarter, they went, flailing away furiously. Beban moved the Bruins 65 yards in seven plays to 20–14. He hit four passes on the drive and the fourth one went to Nuttall 20 yards for the touchdown as the Bruin fans came to their feet screaming and the Trojan fans hunched over in despair.

But the game still hung in the balance, especially after Andrusyshyn, desperately determined to get the ball up over Hayhoe, tried, but failed, as Hayhoe, desperately determined to be a hero, reached and tipped the ball just enough to send it sailing wide.

The miss meant a touchdown and extra point could yet win for USC. And they stood and chanted, "O.J., O.J. All the way with O.J."

He was, as usual, ripping through the line for short gains, getting tackled down, lying there as though hurt or exhausted, getting up slowly, walking slowly and apparently painfully back to the huddle, seemingly unable to make one more run effectively, then taking the ball and making yet another run effectively. His sore foot throbbed terribly, but he was, as usual, running and running and running, wearing down his bigger foes, waiting for that one opening.

Time was running out. The sun was sinking, the light was dimming, a cool wind was whipping away the warmth. The tension had been strung thin, set to snap at any instant. The fans pleaded their highest hopes, the great crowd there and the massive television audience beyond gripped by the climactic moments of this epic battle.

On third down with 8 yards to go from his own 36-yard line, an obvious passing situation, USC quarterback Page called for a short pass to Ron Drake in hopes of gaining a first down that would get a drive rolling. However, as he got to the line of scrimmage, Page saw a UCLA linebacker, anticipating the call, drifting over to provide double coverage on the end, Drake.

Bent over center, Page looked left and right and loudly called the signals to alert his side to a substitute play, 23-Blast, which was Simpson running right, then cutting left between tackle and guard. All Page hoped was to spring Simpson for the first down.

Page barked his signals. The ball was thrust into his hands. He wheeled and handed it off to Simpson, who faked a run to the right, then swerved to the left where tackle Mike Taylor and guard Steve Lehmer had blocked the defenders back, opening a hole in the line.

Simpson exploded through the hole and veered to his left as center Dick Allmon blocked down the linebacker on that side. End Ron Drake screened off the defensive back as Simpson angled back toward the middle, running right through one tackler, then another.

Suddenly an almost open field loomed in front of him. Safety Sandy Grady got a hand on him, but one hand wasn't enough. Simpson shook it off, and running for the right corner, turned on his 9.4-second speed for the 100 yards and raced the last of the 64 yards of this run beyond being caught by the pursuing foes.

As he ran into the end zone, half the stadium was screaming and the other half was silent. Three hours into his tenth game of his spectacular season, after taking terrible punishment, on a flawed foot, Simpson had turned in, not his longest, but his most sensational and meaningful run, for it had tied this crucial contest and set the stage for his side to win it and all that went with it, which they did when Aldridge converted for the 21–20 triumph.

"The thrill of it," Bob Oates later wrote, "will last to the last day of the last man alive who saw it."

UCLA could not come back. The gun barked and the Bruins hung their heads in the bitter disappointment only young athletes understand and walked slowly off, while the Trojans surged around Simpson and Coach McKay and hugged them and pounded their backs and turned to congratulating one another as their supporters stood in the increasing darkness and cheered them off. They whooped and hollered their way into the dressing room, where a washed-out McKay called the big play of the biggest game, "a great call and the greatest run."

Sore and soiled and sweaty, Simpson sat by his locker smiling as the reporters and broadcasters poured all over him and he looked up, his eyes twinkling, and he said, "I got the call and I got the hole and I got the other blocks and I just got going. It was a good run, yes, but it was a team thing. The whole game was a team effort." And he kept refusing credit and spreading it around and he kept smiling.

"It was my biggest thrill," he said. "I can't imagine anything will ever top this."

And years later he would say, "Nothing has ever topped that one."

Ninety minutes later, showered and splendid in civvies, Simpson and Beban met in the dark tunnel outside the dressing rooms. Simpson had run thirty times for 177 yards. Beban had passed twenty-four times for 301 yards. Simpson had run for more than 1,400 yards on the season. Beban had passed for more than 1,300 yards with a game to go. What could they say to each other?

O.J. said, "Gary, you're the greatest."

Gary said, "O.J., you're the best."

O.J. said, "It's too bad one of us had to lose."

Gary said, "Go get 'em in the Rose Bowl."

And they walked away their separate ways.

Beban had lost the biggest game, but he won the Heisman Trophy. He was a senior and Simpson only a junior and the selectors usually favor the fellow who will have no more chances. Simpson would win it the next season, when he would run his two-year total to an NCAA record for rushers of more than 3,400 yards. He would "get 'em" in the Rose Bowl, too, a winner at the end of that first season, a loser the next season, but star and Most Valuable Player of both New Year's Day classics.

And while Beban would try and fail and try again and fail again and try again and fail finally to make it as a pro, Simpson, following a controversial holdout for a prodigious payoff, would struggle through several seasons with a terrible team, in Buffalo, but he would make it, before finally rising to superstardom in the National Football League such as he had enjoyed in high school and junior college and senior college.

He would be voted the greatest college football player of his decade, who may become the greatest runner pro football has had.

He is a player who stands apart from most. And a person who stands apart from the rest.

2 "Pencil-Pins"

Orenthel James Simpson was born on the ninth of July, 1947, in Stanford University Hospital in Palo Alto. He was the second of four children born to Jimmy and Eunice Simpson. There was an older sister, Shirley, and, later, a younger sister, Carmelita, and a younger brother, Leon.

"I was given the name Orenthel by an aunt, who suggested it to my mother," O.J. smiles. "She tagged her own children with names such as Stewart and James." His father laughs and adds, "God knows where she got it." His mother says, "I think that there was a French actor or somethin' called that and she liked it."

O.J. says, "As soon as I was old enough to understand, I made it 'O.J.' Just 'O.J.' There was no way I was going to go around being called 'Orenthel.' There is no way of even shortening it to give me a nickname. I could have used my middle name but that was my dad's name, too, and I didn't want to be called 'Junior.' So I became just 'O.J.'

"And it's been good for me. It's special. It stands out. Later on, it helped make me famous. I think as O.J. Simpson I became more outstanding to the press and public than I would have been as Orenthel Simpson or Jimmy Simpson. Some people sometimes have called me 'Orange Juice,' of course. And some have written it that way. But not too much. It hasn't stuck, really. I'm just O.J."

He was reared in San Francisco. His father, a custodian for the Federal Reserve Bank of San Francisco from the time O.J. was a little boy, and later proprietor of his own catering business, and his mother separated when O.J. was five. His mother worked as an orderly in a hospital while she raised her three children.

The family moved often, usually into old apartment houses or government housing developments. "I remember lots of places," O.J. said. "But mostly I remember Connecticut Street on Potrero Hill. That's where we were in my high school years." He calls it, smilingly, "your average black ghetto."

Most of the places they lived were slum areas, poor places, full of poor blacks or Orientals. The Simpsons were poor. Before he was a year old O.J. began to suffer from a calcium deficiency in his legs, which probably represented rickets. He had to wear braces for years and when the braces came off he was left with thin and bowed legs.

His mother says, "He was a fat baby, but when he was nine months old and trying to walk we noticed he was having trouble with his legs, which seemed weak, so we took him to a doctor, who said he didn't have enough calcium. He said it might have been rickets. So he prescribed some stuff for him and put him in braces. That's why his legs bowed."

So, a baby who could not walk grew up to become a great runner.

"It didn't seem likely at first," O.J. recalls. "My legs were so skinny the other kids nicknamed me 'Pencilpins.' I didn't like them teasing me, but my legs were thin as pencils. They still are thin and still are slightly bowed. But they're strong now. They're not the typical thick, muscular legs of a runner, but maybe they are a sprinter's legs. In any event, they support me just fine. They get the job done."

He grew up defiant and tough among defiant and tough kids in his definitely tough neighborhoods. He said, "I was in a lot of street fights. Maybe because I usually won. I was proud I was a tough scrapper. We had our gangs. They were full of guys who didn't know right from wrong and couldn't have cared less. They stole things and mugged guys and got locked up and got sent away a lot.

"I stole—hubcaps and things. But as a kid I was more a talker than a doer. I'd say, 'Hey, let's do this.' Others were the doers. They'd do it and get caught by the cops. I did some things, but I was lucky and wasn't caught much. I was hauled in as a juvenile offender a couple of times, but that's about all. I was arrested for taking part in a rumble once. But I never got the book thrown at me."

Recalling those days with wistful wonder, he said, "I am only fortunate I didn't get into serious trouble before it was too late. We didn't care about anything good. We didn't know anything good. All we knew was what was there, which wasn't good." His wife, Marguerite, who met him in high school, said, "He was a terrible person in those days. Just awful. I sensed something good in him, but I don't think it really showed. He lived on the brink of disaster."

He says, "I started fights and crashed dances. I wanted to show the boys and girls how big a man I was. I couldn't afford a letterman's jacket, so I strutted my stuff in other ways. I was very cocky. When I was jailed after that street fight and the cop asked me my name, I wised off; 'Burt Lancaster.' I guess he didn't think about it. I was proud of myself for fooling him as I watched him write it down in the book.

"Some of the kids I ran around with got hooked on narcotics or crime. If it hadn't been for football, that would've been me. What could I have done? What chance would I have had? I'd have been digging ditches at best.

"I've thought about it and I know I'm the same person now I was then, only I'm more grown-up and got more responsibilities. Through football I was exposed to another way of life. And I liked it. Eventually, I got to making a lot of money. And I liked that.

"I'm basically a nice guy, I think. I like people and try to treat them well. But it's easy when you're on top. If I'd stayed down, the good that was in me might never have come out. I didn't like it being down. I had a lot of hatred and defiance in me. I could easily have come to a bad end if I hadn't gotten a break."

One of his close friends was picked up for pushing marijuana and assaulting a bus driver and did a couple of years in jail. Seeing a picture of his pal in the newspaper, a football star, inspired him to try another way.

O.J. says, "He told me that when he saw my picture he was kind of shook. It took him awhile to realize that I was the same kid he used to run with. He said he sat there thinking if I could make it, maybe he could, too.

He got out and got into a junior college and started to play football, himself. It made me proud, like I'd been an influence for good in someone's life.

"Trouble doesn't have to follow you. If you want to badly enough, you can run away from it."

O.J. ran—with a football under his arm. Though it almost was with a baseball bat in his hand. A cousin of Ernie Banks, he was hooked on all sports. He used to sell programs in Kezar Stadium to see San Francisco 49ers games. Or sneak in or buy half-buck bleacher seats and climb the fence to get into the better sections. "I never missed a game," he has insisted proudly.

He played baseball and basketball and football whenever and wherever he could. He said, "I was one of those little kids who is always recruited to play with the big kids. I guess they wanted me because I could play anything as well as they could."

His mother has said, "Sports, it was always sports with that boy." His father has said, "He was always such an ambitious boy. And not just in athletics, either. You'd buy him a toy and he'd take it apart to see what it was made of. He was always fixing radios and things. But I'll agree that sports came first."

O.J. has said, "Football gave me a way out of my poor life, for which I will forever be grateful to it. But baseball could have been a way out for me, too. Baseball was my first love, though I loved all sports. I don't know how I expected to get to the top. I never even thought of college. I didn't study, and got poor grades. Kids dream, 'I'm good enough.' I was just dreaming."

High school coach Jack McBride says, "O.J. was a very lazy student."

O.J. was a hard-hitting catcher, who also played excellent shortstop and outfield. He captained his junior high school team. But he went to an afternoon school dance one day instead of to practice and he was put off the team.

"I kept playing here and there, but not seriously after that," O.J. says. "I let it get to me. But I could have been a good baseball player I think, and probably a pro."

He went to Galileo High School, which had a proud sports history, having produced Joe DiMaggio, the great baseball star; Hank Luisetti, the immortal basketball performer, who revolutionized the game with his one-handed shot, and Lawson Little, a former professional champion golfer.

However, by the time O.J. got to Galileo, its student body was composed primarily of Orientals, who were mostly small. At 160 pounds, O.J. seemed enormous to his new coaches. His first coaches, the junior varsity coaches, McBride and George Poppin, promptly made him into a tackle.

McBride admits, "The first time we saw him move, we saw we might have made a mistake." He was soon moved into the defensive backfield, which was a mistake, too. Later, he was a receiver before he became a runner, which was a mistake, too. He was a receiver as much as a runner throughout high school.

While still on the JV's, he was far from reformed. One day Coach McBride walked into the lavatory and found O.J. and two other players shooting dice on the day of a big game. He sent them to the dean's office.

Later, O.J. recalled, "McBride, a white guy, was a

guy I respected more than anybody in the world. Instead of letting us go and saying, 'Let's play the game and don't do it again,' he turned us into the dean. And even though I felt bad about it at the time and I was a little mad at him, he told me that no one was going to give me anything in this world. He said, 'If you want something, you'll have to work for it and act like you deserve it. You know, if you want respect you're going to have to act respectable.' And that's something I've never forgotten. I think it's helped me and I'll always be grateful to him for turning me in to the dean."

Even though it caused him to miss the game? O.J. giggled and said, "I didn't miss the game. I lied and got out of it. When we went to the dean's office, the two other guys—Joe Bell, who played at the University of Washington, and Al Cowlings, who played at USC with me—walked in in front of me. Coach McBride told the dean he'd caught these students playing dice in the rest room. He gave the dean the dice and left. I started out, too, and began to close the door behind me. The dean called, 'Where are you going, O.J.?' I said, 'I wasn't shooting craps. Coach just asked me to help him bring these guys down.' So the dean told me I could go. And I went," he laughed.

"And when the coach asked me if I'd been suspended, I said, 'No,' so I played. The other guys were suspended. And they respected me for it. They thought it was pretty smart of me to think that quick. That's the way we thought in those days. Al said there was nothing he could say about it. He said if I could get away with that, I deserved it. I still remember what the coach said, though. I got away lucky, but it made a deep impression on me. I started to straighten out some."

O.J. moved up to the varsity, but the team was terrible and went 0–9 his junior season. Larry McInerney, who'd had great success as a coach at St. Ignatius, took over the team the following season. Galileo hadn't won in three years. After three more games in O.J.'s senior season, it still hadn't won. And then they had to take on St. Ignatius, which hadn't lost in two years. McInerney was hopeful of upsetting his old team, but he also was a realist and he figured if his side took another beating he'd stop playing the seniors and start playing the sophomores and juniors, who were his hopes for the future.

O.J. has recalled, "We were on the team bus when the coach said that if we didn't beat St. Ignatius he would put the seniors on the bench for the rest of the season and play only juniors and sophomores. I was sitting next to Al Cowlings and I remember telling Cowlings, 'I don't care if we lose or not, do you?' And he turned to me and said, 'So what?' And I said, 'So what' right back to him. It's sad, but we weren't used to winning, we didn't expect to win, and we didn't have any deep dedication."

Still, when he played, he played hard. He was playing defensive back and running back kicks and catching passes. St. Ignatius led in the fourth quarter when Simpson ranged far across the field to steal the ball from the runner, Dave McFarland, and raced 60 yards to an unexpected and critical score. It was his third touchdown of the half and led Galileo to a stunning 31–26 upset victory.

"It wasn't so hard," O.J. recalled. "The man with the ball was being hit by two men. As he went down, he reached forward with his arms and the ball in an effort to get more yardage. I just grabbed the ball right out of his hands and ran like hell with it." McInerney has recalled, "It was a super play and a super run and it really opened our eyes. We saw we had to use him more running.

"I could say that I'm the smartest coach ever. But I have to be truthful. O.J. would have made good no matter who was coaching him. He had great natural talent, which had to come out. He was not only fast, but he was tough, very tough.

"O.J.'s senior year, our passer was the third leading passer, statistically, in the conference. But that was deceiving. He'd give O.J. a five-yard screen pass and O.J. would run seventy-five yards with it. From scrimmage, O.J. was just developing, but when we could spring him loose, he was strong. With him, we began to win."

The team won five of its last six games to finish at 5–4, which was considered remarkable for Galileo considering what sort of records it had been putting together. "I tried to run over people like Jim Brown did in pro ball," Simpson has said. "It didn't work for me. I learned to be my own man. I learned a lot at Galileo."

Years later, when he was honored at this ancient school in ceremonies in which "O.J. Simpson Football Field" was dedicated, O.J. smiled and wisecracked, "Since I spent most of my years here in the dean's office I figured that's what they would name after me."

Remembering the many visits he made to that office

and especially that one visit when he was almost suspended for shooting dice and the time he was kicked off his junior high baseball team, he once observed, "If I'd been kicked off my high school football team, I'd have quit school, and I really don't believe much could have come of me. Football was the real reason I stayed in school and I came really very close to losing out on it and everything that went with it and followed it, and I wonder sometimes how many guys went that way, wasting themselves."

Shaking his head, smiling wistfully, he observed, "Colleges began to come after me then, despite my bad grades. I hadn't been such a hotshot that everyone wanted me, but some must have seen the sort of potential I had because they expressed interest in helping me so they could get me. All of a sudden I could see I might get into college and I began to wonder if I could get by somehow and I began to look ahead to playing pro ball and making some kind of fantastic living as an athlete. I wasn't stupid. I just wasn't well schooled or sophisticated. I hadn't worked at it and I was starting from behind the eight ball. But out of nowhere the chance was there and I had only to reach out to take it."

3 O.J. in JC

O.J. was not actively recruited by the major college football forces until after his first season at San Francisco City College in junior college ranks. He even considered enlisting in the Army. Offered an opportunity to attend this school and with low grades that needed to be raised if he was to qualify for a major university, he grabbed the chance to further himself in football.

Before he enrolled, some San Francisco newsmen were teasing the Galileo graduate that he couldn't make the City College team. "I can't, huh? I'll prove it to you," Simpson snapped, rising to the bait.

Sam Skinner, well-known black sportswriter in the area, recalls: "He registered at the last possible moment. He made the team, all right. For two weeks, he was a defensive back. Until all the running backs got hurt. The next week they used him on offense. He scored four touchdowns. He was a runner forever after."

He scored twenty-six touchdowns his first season at San Francisco City and twenty-eight his second season. He ran for six touchdowns in one game—on runs of 88, 73, 58, 16, and 14 yards and a catch-and-run of 27 yards. He had other runs of 97, 95, and 85 yards. He not only ran from scrimmage, but he ran with pass-catches and he ran with punts and kickoffs and in difficult defensive situations he played defensive back. He rushed for more than 2,500 yards and his fifty-four touchdowns surpassed Ollie Matson's school record. He was simply sensational and he led his team to eighteen consecutive victories at one stretch and to the top of the junior college rankings and to two JC bowl games and twice was selected JC All-America.

His coach there, Dutch Elston, says, "Later I heard John McKay say USC helped teach Simpson how to run. I want to tell you something: Nobody taught that boy how to run. Trying to teach him how to run would be like trying to teach Bing Crosby or Ray Charles how to sing. We just left him alone. We tried to fit him into an offensive pattern and put him in places where he could use his skills the best, and he learned fast, but as a runner he was a natural.

"He simply did more things than any other runners. He had unusual speed for a man his size, great balance, and a knack for escaping tacklers. He got through holes quick, but he could find his own holes. He had an instinct about the best ways to go. He had peripheral vision to the degree he could see the whole scene laid out around him. He could anticipate the force of a tackle coming to him and he could survive. He could absorb a blow and have the ability to go off on a tangent and get away. And he was physically tough. He never was incapacitated while playing more than twenty games for us.

"We played him a lot of places. He gained most of his yardage and scored most of his touchdowns running from scrimmage, but he was effective outside as a wide receiver and so much of a threat there he made our inside offense go. He ran back kicks because he was always a threat to go all the way. In sticky situations we even used him a little at defensive back because he was the best. He could have made it in nine positions on any level—at the two or three running-back spots, at the two or three receiving spots, and at the four defensive backfield spots—and he still could.

"We never were so deep in talent we could afford not using him in a lot of spots. He never complained about where we put him or how much we used him. He just wanted to play. He was very intense in his desire to play football. And he was a leader. I think I remember more than any other game a game against Chabot JC in 1966 in which they had us by six at halftime and O.J. talked to the team in the locker room and stirred them up and went out and broke a seventy-yarder at the start of the second half and lifted the team so it just ran away with the game.

"We happened to turn up other good players to go with him. Mike Taylor played with him in 1965 and Al Cowlings, Ruby Jackson, and Bob Lee in 1966. Taylor and Cowlings went on to play pro, too. Jackson went on to play pro in Canada. Lee became a pro quarterback with Minnesota. I know O.J. understood even a player as good as he was needed help. I talked to him about this. And I think it helped influence him to go to USC, where he got good blocking and was surrounded by good offensive players.

"He probably understands it more than ever now that he has had to struggle for success in pro ball with teammates in Buffalo who are mostly not as good as their rivals. He is the same player with less help and so he has not looked as good, but he is still the greatest.

"We probably had our greatest teams here with him, although they'd had great teams here before, such as when they had Matson, who was magnificent. With Ollie, I think they won twelve in a row. I hadn't had any such teams here until O.J. arrived. We lost the first game of his first season, to L.A. Valley. Then we won all the rest, including the big game that decided the conference crown against San Jose JC, which is the game in which O.J. exploded for six scores. They'd only lost one and they were good, but he beat them bad almost all by himself.

"We were invited to, of all names, The Prune Bowl, in San Jose, and we played Long Beach City College, which had a top team with players like Earl McCullouch, who later was O.J.'s star teammate at USC and then became a pro star with the Detroit Lions. They had a strong squad, but we beat them by something like forty to twenty with Simpson standing out. We wound up nine and one.

"The next season, O.J.'s last season, we wound up nine and one, too, to make our record eighteen and two during his stay here. We won our first nine to run our winning streak to eighteen straight, but then we returned to the Prune Bowl in San Jose and lost to Laney JC by about thirty-one to thirteen. We didn't expect to play in the game, we didn't scout them at all, Laney was loaded, and we went in without being ready to play our best.

"Maybe we should have appeared in the Junior Rose Bowl in Pasadena they used to play and draw big crowds and great attention, but the sponsors figured the biggest payoff came when they had a 'home' team from southern California playing a visitor from far away like Texas or Oklahoma and it did work for them so we never were invited. Maybe our players were a little disappointed.

"O.J. made a fine impression here and on me and he certainly was the best player I ever coached, though I can't take much credit for his development.

"I know he was supposed to be a tough and troubled youngster when he arrived, but he didn't give any outward appearance of it, except maybe for one instance. He ran on our track team. In fact, he was a member of a record-setting relay unit. But after his first football season he got into a beef with a teammate from the football team and he belted him in the head and broke his hand and it affected his track because you can't run real good with a heavy cast on one hand. But he had recovered from it by the time the football season rolled around again and he was ready to run effectively the following spring in track before he graduated.

"He wasn't real aggressive in his relations with others, usually. He could talk, but he was always a better listener than a talker. He was attentive, sensitive, diplomatic. He could interrogate you without you realizing it. He was very pliable, himself. And he had a way of shaping others. He's really a charming, persuasive person. He was then and he still is now. His 'antennas' are always out. He plays it cool, but he knows what's going on around him and he never seems to be out of place. He can make things work for him. He's really a remarkable individual and I think the unusual things he has inside him have helped make him into a fine football player as well as a fine person.

"He overcame a lot," concludes Dutch Elston. "He was under a lot of pressure even while he was here and he had to make some hard decisions about how he was going to reshape his life, but he made good ones."

After Simpson averaged between 11 and 12 yards a carry his freshman season, the big schools began to bear down on him. Most of the Pacific Eight and Big Ten universities sent scouts to court him, as did many major independents. USC, Notre Dame, and Ohio State were among the name schools which sought him seriously. The University of California at Berkeley was a local college which really romanced him. However, his grades still were not good enough for entrance into most of these schools. Utah and Arizona State were universities which were prepared to enroll him immediately. And he was tempted.

Simpson had become a University of Southern California fan after the 1962 season when the Trojans went unbeaten and untied in eleven games and won the national championship. After seeing the USC club hang on to trim Wisconsin, 42–38, in a remarkable Rose Bowl contest, he was hooked. Then, when a brilliant running-back, Mike Garrett, burst into headlines in 1963 with 833 yards running and in 1964 with 948 yards running and climaxed his career in 1965 with 1,440 yards and a lifetime total of 3,221 yards and won the Heisman Trophy, O.J. was hooked. That following summer he had to decide which way to go.

"I wanted to play for the best and I thought USC was the best," he said. "I wanted to succeed Mike Garrett as a Trojan. Cal wasn't doing all that much. The Washington and Oregon schools seemed too far away. The Midwest schools seemed too far away. I really just wanted to go to USC. But when they told me they couldn't take me right away and I'd have to stay another year at City College playing junior college ball, I got discouraged. I was anxious to get going in real competition.

"Arizona State and Utah sounded good to me although they were far off because I could have gone to either one and started playing ball right away. I was ready to go to Utah. I went up there and said, 'I'm happy to be going to Utah State.' I didn't know anything. I was really embarrassed. It's funny, but it soured me. There wasn't any way I could go there then. I didn't even know the name of the school. I was really green.

"I almost accepted Arizona State's offer. That was one school which wanted me right out of high school but the coach backed out at the last minute because my grades weren't good enough. Maybe his backing out then weighed against the school later. But I was really ready. But USC assistants Jim Stangeland and Marv Goux kept after me to hang on.

"Goux especially kept talking to me. And that man can talk. He finally said, 'Admit to yourself, O.J., that you really want to come to SC.' I did. And I realized that was what I really wanted. I just didn't want to wait out another year in City College in JC ball. But I decided finally to do that. And I'm glad I did.

"Oh, I'd have become a pretty good player wherever I'd have gone. Arizona State, for example, has had some great runners and I'm sure I could have done my share of running there. I'd probably have run up even more yardage there than I was to at USC. I'd have had one more varsity year and the competition wouldn't have been as tough.

"On the other hand, I probably wouldn't have had the tremendous blocking I did at SC. And I might not have felt inspired by the sort of spirit we had at SC. It's one thing to play for a good team and another to play for a great team. It's inspiring to be at the top of the polls and to be beating the best. It gives you a lot of pride and helps your performances.

"Also, I wouldn't have been in the spotlight at Utah or Arizona State. The best players they ever had there just never attracted that much attention. Los Angeles is the best city in the country for a college football player. Oh, a top player is going to get attention at Notre Dame or Texas or such schools, but L.A. is the biggest city in the country with top college football teams and there is so much press and radio and TV there it gives a big boost to a top player.

"If I'd done at Arizona State or Utah what I did at USC, people might still have doubted me and it's possible I never would have won the Heisman playing at those other schools. In fact, it's probable. You not only have to be a top player, but on a top team, in top competition, and in the spotlight and well publicized to win that trophy. People felt I proved myself at SC.

"So I'm thankful I decided to wait for SC. I've prayed a lot about that. I was guided right in my decision."

One of the things that influenced him was a telephone call from Willie Mays. It came that summer of 1966 when he had graduated from San Francisco City College and remained uncertain which way to go.

Simpson says, "I had waited, but it still wasn't an easy decision. I majored in criminology at City College and it was interesting and my grades got up, but I still worried it might be stiff scholastically at a bigger school like USC than it would be at Arizona State or Utah. I don't know that's so but I thought it was, which is all that mattered.

"And although I had confidence in my ability, I was a little leery about getting lost in the shuffle at SC, where they recruit so many great players. The coaches at Arizona State and Utah warned me about that. They said I could play right away at their schools and might never get to play at the other school. And they were right, too. Not in my case. I made it right off. But I saw a lot of great players who could have starred on lesser teams stuck on the bench at SC. It just didn't happen to me.

"Then came this call from Willie Mays. I still don't know why he called except that he's a fine man and may have read about my indecision and may have felt he could have a positive influence on me. It was like getting a call from a god. He was one of my idols when I was growing up in San Francisco. He always seemed to me not only a great athlete who always put out, but a person with a lot of common sense. After I talked with him, I knew more than ever I was a Willie Mays man.

"He told me I had a very special football ability and I should see this and make the most of it and capitalize on it. He said I shouldn't be afraid to test myself against the best and prove I was the best. He said if someone was the best but didn't think they were they never would become as good as they should be and I had to have confidence in myself and shoot for the top.

"He also talked to me about the people I was sure to encounter along the way—the sincere ones, the insincere ones, the hero-worshippers, the phonies, the do-gooders, the crooks, the camp followers. He said I might become famous at my sport and I should try to treat people decently but I should not allow myself to be pushed around and should be selective in picking people I trusted to be friends.

"He said I owed an obligation to the kids to set an example for them by living decently. He said I might make a lot of money but I owed an obligation to my future to get good advice and handle it carefully. And he said even if I made a million I should not forget my mother and my family and my friends and the people who had helped me along the way.

"It was very inspiring. I was still very young and very unsure of myself and I had a lot of respect for a man who'd been there, at the top, who'd proven himself and had lived something of the sort of life I was likely to lead, and I listened to him, and thanked him, and thought a lot about what he'd said and it had a lot of influence on my thinking.

"I decided for sure I was going to go to USC. And almost as soon as I got there I got married and settled down. I changed my major to public administration, thinking I might go into public service, probably youth work later, after football. I had calmed down. I was no longer a criminal. I was serious about the future. And I staked my future on my football."

He grinned. "Let's face it, the competition I faced in JC ball just wasn't all that tough. Some places it's tougher, but if it had been tougher where I was I could never have broken off so many long runs. I got to where I got to gambling a lot going for long runs.

"There are different ways to run, you know. You can go straight and hard for every yard, looking for the first down first, or you can go around and around, circling around and looking for room to break off a long run while risking getting thrown for a long loss. Well, I got to looking for the long ones and I got them so often, I got sort of cocky.

"I figured, why not USC, why not the best? I figured I was the best, so why not? It was so easy where I had been I figured it couldn't be all that much harder where I was going. Well, I found out it was a lot tougher at the top. But I also found out I was equal to it. I don't mean to sound cocky about it. At the top, it's so tough you need a lot of help. I got it at USC. And I was good enough to use it right.

"I'm glad I waited for USC and I'm glad I went there, finally."

O.J. enrolled at the sprawling city campus, promptly changed with marriage the former Marguerite Whitley into the new Mrs. Simpson, and settled into an apartment a few blocks from campus along with Harvey, a parrakeet who squawked a lot, and an unnamed rubber spider, immensely ugly, who guarded the entrance.

"I keep the spider by the door to ward off evil spirits," O.J. grinned. "I have the parrakeet to keep Marguerite company while I'm on road trips." And Marguerite said, "And I'm going to get a girl parrakeet to keep him company. I'm going to get Harvey a wife. We'll call her Mildred. Harvey and Mildred, how about that!"

O.J. screwed up his face, then laughed and said, "I

don't know how Harvey feels about marriage, but I feel fine about it. I found me a good wife and I look forward to having a fine family. I'm going to be a family man and a homebody."

Quiet and reserved, the new Mrs. Simpson said, "I hope to be a steadying influence on him. He's changed already, but I don't know that I changed him. With all the public attention he's been getting from football, he's become more occupied. It's given him something to do and a sense of responsibility. He's no longer the terrible person he was when I first met him."

O.J. laughed and said, "I don't think I was that terrible. If I was, a good girl like you would never have had anything to do with me."

She said, "I guess I saw some good in you."

"But you had to look hard."

"Real hard, Simpson, real hard."

He laughed.

He hunched over a little, sitting on a couch, and looked down at his large hands and said, "Now all I have to do is make something of myself, starting with football. Now I really have to prove myself as a player."

He came to Los Angeles with a lot of advance publicity, but he had performed in northern California, not southern California, and his teammates and the coaches and the press and the public, who'd had great stars performing in the area over the years, had adopted a wait-and-see attitude toward this latest "phenomenon."

USC had in its past not only Mike Garrett, but C.R. Roberts, Jon Arnett, Frank Gifford, Orv Mohler, Cotton Washburn, and Morley Drury as great running backs. UCLA had Bill Kilmer, Bob Davenport, Paul Cameron, Kenny Washington, and Jack Robinson as renowned runners in its history. The pro Rams had Dick Bass, still making miracles, and Arnett, Tommy Wilson, Ron Waller, Tank Younger, Dan Towler, Tom Harmon, and Washington remembered as super-runners of other days.

Simpson was just another prospect, and was suspect.

In spring training, head coach John McKay decided to test him right off. McKay recalls, "We knew he was fast and could run, but he'd run outside a lot in JC ball and we wanted to see if he could take it inside. So, in scrimmage, we ran him seven straight times. And that was it. He just busted people backwards. We knew we had someone special then.

"And we were even more certain when we saw how quick he got to holes and through them and how well he used his blockers and the sort of moves he had and the size and strength and unusual speed he had when he got into a broken field or an open field. We tried to keep it to ourselves.

"We knew he'd been getting publicity and would get a lot more and we wanted to hold it down within reason if we could, but we couldn't. He showed too good too soon. Luckily, he was able to handle it."

Sighs McKay, "Even we didn't know how good he really was. We saw he was very good. But we didn't realize he was great. Not right off. Maybe we suspected what he might be, but we were afraid to believe it at first. We just went with him and began to use him more and more and the more we asked of him the more we got out of him. He was sensational, of course."

4 O.J. at USC

John McKay is a very funny man, perhaps the funniest coach in competition today. He is quick. The lines are not thought out in advance. They come naturally. And they are funny. When a runner stumbled and fell after running only 5 yards with the opening kickoff, McKay screamed from the sidelines, "My God, they've shot him!"

Taking credit for a series of last-minute victories one season, McKay commented, "My system is that my quarterback runs the game for fifty-nine minutes, then I take over the last minute."

Disdaining blame after a few close losses, McKay introduced his assistant coaches at a banquet: "Take a good look at these men. After all, everyone knows we get the best talent. And everyone knows I'm a good coach. Someone must be to blame for failure. So this may be the last time you see these men."

Of course, he is paid to win games, not to be funny. And he was a winner, but he sometimes lost and the funny line could conceal the disappointment. The year before Simpson enrolled at USC, the Trojans won seven of eleven games, but one of the losses was shocking, 51–0, to Notre Dame. Afterward, McKay entered the locker room and confronted his dejected team and said, "Don't worry men, there are five hundred million Chinese who will never know the difference."

Everyone knows the fast tongue. Few know the man behind it. He hides behind it. In a rare reflective moment he admitted, "Sometimes I'm laughing on the outside, crying on the inside. I guess I have a sense of humor. I try not to take things too seriously. I try to put pain in perspective. But when you're feeling real pain, like after a tough loss, my jokes are some sort of defense mechanism, I guess. I have to say something to the press. If I can give 'em a fast line, that's all they ask. They'll take it and go away with it and leave me alone.

"The games are easier on the player. He has other interests. Afterwards, he goes out. He goes to a party. He goes out with a girl. He forgets. He escapes. But the game is the coach's life. He carries it around with him. The games you've played and the games you've got to play. There's no escaping them. And your job depends on your winning.

"You have to have a sense of where you are. We're a good school. The school has to come first. We send more players into pro ranks than anyone else, but most of our players still aren't going to make pro and they have to be prepared for it. But the football staff doesn't teach English and science. We teach football. Football is getting most of our players through college and they have a responsibility to it. And we teach winning here. But you can't tell your players it's a matter of life and death, even if it is to the coach. Our approach is, we want to win, but if we lose, life goes on. Win or lose, the guys have to be in class on Monday.

"So you have to do your best to keep it reasonable.

That's why I'm not much for impassioned pep talks. I'd rather kid 'em and keep 'em loose. I don't want to be responsible for any suicides later. In 1964, we came from zero to seventeen in the first half to beat Notre Dame twenty to seventeen in the second half. People asked me what I said at halftime to inspire 'em so. I said, 'Listen, if you don't score more than seventeen points in the second half you're gonna' get your rear end beat.' "

McKay, in his forties, gray-haired, but tanned, fit and healthy looking, had come from hard times as a boy in West Virginia, where he starred in football and basketball. He went into World War II where he was a tail gunner, emerged to play one year at Purdue, then transferred to Oregon, where he completed his college career as an all-coast halfback and teammate of Norm Van Brocklin's.

His quick mind and willingness to work impressed head coach Jim Aiken, who retained him as an aide. After eight years, USC hired him away as an assistant to Don Clark and less than a year later he replaced Clark as head man. That was in 1960. After two losing years, he put together his undefeated national champion Rose Bowl winner in 1962 and has not had a loser since.

However, he had been losing two or three games a year and losing out on the conference crown and the Rose Bowl berth for four years before Simpson arrived. He had lost to archrival UCLA and its new coach Tommy Prothro two years in a row. And he had lost out on the bowl bid until the year before O.J. came on when his team reluctantly was awarded a berth in Pasadena, where USC was nosed out by Purdue, 14–13. Just having been there, however, helped make up O.J.'s mind. He wanted to go to a team that went to the big bowl.

Despite his wisecracking, McKay was and is a tough man, who once observed, "I've checked my heart. I don't have one." He has said, "Coaching is a tough profession and you have to be tough to endure it. You take a lot from your family." His wife, Corky, goes to his games, but is too nervous to watch them. She usually paces in the tunnel leading into the stands. A new usher once started to chase her. A knowing usher stopped him. He said, "Leave her alone. She's been in this tunnel so many years she owns it by now."

McKay has been criticized by some observers and by some of his players for not getting closer to them personally or treating them gently. He shrugs and says, "With eighty guys on a football team and a complete turnover every two to four years, you don't have time to get to know them as people as much as you'd like. My job is to get to know them as players and I can't wet-nurse them. But I'm always available to them and so are the other coaches. We'd rather have them respect us than love us."

His top assistant has been Marv Goux, a great lineman and linebacker from Santa Barbara, who starred at USC in the early 1950's despite being small of stature, twice won the award given annually to the most inspirational player, graduated into an assistant coaching spot, and stayed to become the most inspirational coach on the staff. He often has taken over the halftime speeches for McKay because McKay sees Goux as a more emotional man who rouses the players with his peptalks. And he has been a persuasive recruiter who talked the much-sought-after Simpson into becoming a Trojan.

Simpson says, "They're a terrific team. There is no question who is the head man. McKay rules with a firm hand. He is firm, but fair. He is tough, but not brutal. He is a very funny man, but he knows when it's time to laugh and when it's time to be serious. He keeps things in the proper perspective. And he is a good coach. He has a brilliant mind and he goes for broke. He's not afraid to gamble. He's a winner. He has confidence and he gives you confidence. I don't go along with those who think he's distant. I always felt close to him. It wasn't a matter of being buddy-buddy or anything. Or a matter of me being important to him. He treated me the same as he treated others. But I respected him.

"Goux was just great. He has the ability to be a top head man, but he is an unbelievably good assistant. He does a big job, but never oversteps his position. He has a gift of gab that is just unbelievable. And he is some fighter. He charms you and he challenges you and he stirs you up. His locker-room talks are partly responsible for the tremendous spirit I felt at USC. I've never felt anything like it anywhere else. It wasn't just because we won. The spirit made us win. And it has stuck to us. We really felt loyalty to USC. We became proud to be Trojan football players. And we miss it once we're away from the team and we worry about the team and root for it.

"They get so many good players there that it's tough on some who don't get to play. It's not that they recruit too much. They don't give out any more scholarships than anyone else. They don't pay off on the side or under the table. But when you're a winner, guys want to go to your school and it's easy for them to get top talent. And I'm sure they regret it when good guys are squeezed out of the lineup. And they just have to live with the hurt feelings that follow. So there are some guys who are not happy with the situation. But USC recruits very selectively. They've turned a lot of players who were not high school stars and widely sought into good performers who were just what they needed. My teams were just tremendous. I wouldn't have been half as effective as I was without the help I got. They freed me to do my thing."

Simpson was just what USC needed. The Trojans had competent but not brilliant quarterbacks in Toby Page and Steve Sogge and outstanding receivers in tight-end Bob Klein and wide men Earl "The Pearl" McCullouch and Jim Lawrence, but they lacked a strong runner. Offensively, giant tackle Ron Yary anchored an excellent line of blockers. Defensively, ends Tim Rossovich and Jim Gunn, linebackers Adrian Young and Jim Snow and defensive back Mike Battle bulwarked an all-star cast. Simpson, Yary, and Young would win all-American honors, while they, Klein and McCullouch eventually would be high pro draft picks and pro regulars.

Simpson, who enrolled in February of 1967, got in only seven days of spring practice because he wanted to compete as a sprinter with the fine Trojan track team. A sprinter who ran the 100 yards in 9.4 seconds at his best, O.J. finished sixth in the NCAA championship 100 and joined McCullouch on the four-man 440-yard relay team which sizzled to a world record 38.6 clocking. His speed spotlighted him before his football did. But by the fall when the new season began, he hit the headlines in a hurry. He fitted in with the team fast and earned a regular's role from the start.

The Trojans opened at home against Washington State and had no trouble walloping the Cougars, 49–0. O.J. ran seventeen times for 94 yards and caught a couple of passes for 28 more yards. He had one 40 yard run recalled on a penalty.

The first real test came the following week against visiting Texas. More than 67,000 fans turned out on a warm Saturday night to see the meeting of the two top-rated teams, and it was a splendid contest.

USC drove deep into Texas territory at the outset, but Simpson fumbled at the 15, Texas recovered, and touted quarterback Bill Bradley promptly drove Darrell Royal's Longhorns 85 yards to the first touchdown. In the second quarter, Battle took a short punt deep into Texas territory again. Sogge passed to Lawrence for 16 yards to the 9. Then Simpson took it the rest of the way, running inside for 7, then outside for the last 2 to tie the contest.

As the game ground on, Simpson's slashing runs gave his side ball-control, while the Texas running star Chris Gilbert was contained. In the third quarter, Simpson squirted 18 yards up the middle for the big play of a 68-yard drive that put the Trojans on top. Another drive in the last period resulted in a 30-yard field goal by Rikki Aldridge to put the game out of reach. A last-minute Texas touchdown fell short, 17–13.

At the gun, Simpson had run thirty times for 158

yards and caught a pass for another 20 yards and was the star of the show, cheered off the field by the happy home fans. He sat by his locker later, too happy even to get out of his scarlet and gold uniform number 32 and said, "That sure was a lot of fun. Yes, I had a good game. The whole team did." McKay said, "Everyone did play well. They had to to beat a team as tough as Texas. But Simpson was the star."

In the subdued dressing room of the losers, Royal said, "I hope I don't see anybody this season with more capabilities than Simpson. And you know something? I don't think I will." The Houston Oilers' scout Charlie Hall shook his head and said, "I'm glad I don't have to coach against him. He'd scare me to death. Even when he looks bad, he winds up making three yards. I'll tell you, we'll take him right now." Oakland manager Al Davis asked, "Who wouldn't take him? He has everything a great back needs. He's so explosive, nothing can stop him from greatness."

After two games of his first varsity season, Simpson was saluted with a spread in *The Sporting News*. Soon the magazines—*Sport Magazine*, *Sports Illustrated*, and the others—would follow with feature stories and cover pictures. Behind a big buildup, O.J. only had to come through in the first couple of outings to attract attention. But the best was yet to come.

The Trojans invaded East Lansing to take on Michigan State's Spartans, a Big Ten powerhouse, which had been upset the previous weekend by Houston and was hungry. A crowd of more than 75,000 fans filled Spartan Stadium on a cold, overcast Saturday afternoon. The field was spongy from two preceding days of rain, but USC moved across it 71 yards in seven plays the first time it got the ball, to take a 7–0 lead. Simpson ran five times for 57 yards on the drive, finally for 8 yards and the touchdown.

However, early in the second quarter, Battle bobbled a punt on his own 4-yard line, fumbled, and State covered it on the 1 and ran it over one play later to tie. Sogge picked the Spartans apart with passes and Simpson banged over from in close to regain the lead for SC. But Jimmy Raye threw for a 47-yard score to Al Brenner with forty-three seconds left in the half and State added a 2-point conversation to go 1 point ahead. And when Dick Allmon snapped the ball high over punter Aldridge's head and he ran out of the end zone chasing it down, it was a safety and the Spartans were hollered off the field by the happy home folks with a 17–14 edge at the intermission.

Mad about his team's mistakes, McKay in his halftime talk told the Trojans, it was "ridiculous" they were behind. Simpson took the opening kickoff of the second half into a wall of green and white jerseys at the 26 and the Trojans went to work. With Sogge passing and Simpson running, the visitors drove to the Spartan 7 in ten plays. Then Simpson started off running around the right end, which sucked State in, stopped at the corner, and pegged a perfect pass to Lawrence, who was all alone in the end zone, and SC went ahead, 21–17.

With O.J. slashing for short runs, the Trojans controlled the ball a lot the remainder of a tense second half. The Spartans made one drive 70 yards to the Trojan 5, but what appeared to be a touchdown on a pass was nullified by an offensive interference penalty, the ball went back, and State stalled. The home side was never again able to mount so serious a threat and there was no further scoring. When the gun barked in the gathering gloom, the huge home crowd was smothered in gloom.

Sogge had completed fourteen of sixteen passes for 182 yards, but it was Simpson, running thirty-one times for 190 yards, the most ever gained by one runner on the ground against a Michigan State team, running for two scores and throwing for the third, who was the prime subject of the postmortems. Notre Dame scout Joe Yonto said, "Simpson is truly great." Michigan State coach Duffy Daugherty agreed, "He's a great back, a really great back." USC coach McKay allowed, "Well, I think he played rather well. Especially since he had a charley horse all week." Simpson said, "The injury didn't bother me. They did. They hit like Texas. Hard! I ran well. But the blockers blocked even better."

Ranked in the top five in the nation, the Southern Cal crew drew a break in the brutal schedule with one of the lesser Stanford teams arriving in the Coliseum. A crowd of more than 60,000 came out to cheer as the home side coasted home, but O.J. was one who was not given much rest. He carried the ball twenty-nine times for 160 yards, caught two passes for 52 yards, and threw a pass for 9 yards and another touchdown as SC romped, 30–0. McCullouch caught two passes for touchdowns and five others.

The victory was costly, as fullback Mike Hull suffered a knee injury which would sideline him for the season, with Dan Scott moving in, but most of the Trojan running game was in Simpson's hands and legs anyway. Curiously, while he had moved his total up past 600 yards to take the national lead away from Eugene "Mercury" Morris of West Texas State, Simpson had yet to break a big one, his longest in the first four games being a mere 29 yards, not counting the 40-yarder against Washington State, which did not count.

His wife suggested, "O.J., maybe you should throw a few more fakes instead of running so straight." Her husband smiled and said, "She likes long runs." Reflectively, O.J. added, "I do, too. But I'm not going for them. I'm not gambling. I think they'll come, but right now I'm on a team that can march so I go for the first downs first to keep the marches moving and it's paying off. I'm carrying the ball a lot and working hard and picking up the ground in short chunks. We passed all the tests so far, but the biggest yet is coming up."

That was Notre Dame, which had humbled the Trojans 51–0 in the Coliseum the season before. And the Irish, undefeated and rated Number one, were waiting with Terry Hanratty to pass, Jim Seymour to catch, Rocky Bleier to run, and huge Keven Hardy to defend. At home, they were installed a 12-point favorite. McKay suggested, "We may not show up." Someone said, "If you don't, you'll lose by forfeit." McKay asked. "What's the score of a forfeit game?" The reply was, "Two to nothing." McKay smiled and shrugged and said, "Well, that'd be forty-nine points better than we did last year."

But McKay had no intention of giving up. Humiliated as he had been by the landslide loss suffered the previous season, he regarded it as just one of those things which had got out of hand. He knew his side had been better than that and was much better right now and with Simpson he figured he could cut the Irish to ribbons, though he worried that his young team might freeze up moving from warm to cold weather and might choke up in the shadow of the Golden Dome, where visitors were assaulted by a savage home crowd on Saturdays. In fact, the Trojans had not won at South Bend in twenty-eight years, though they had played there almost every other season. "I haven't been here all those twenty-eight years," McKay reminded everyone.

A full house of 59,000 fanatics awaited them, as did the lads in the blue jerseys and gold helmets with the largest line this side of the Chicago Bears. The contest was advertised as the Poll Bowl, the winner presumably getting the number-one ranking in the nation, which Notre Dame held and expected to hold on to. And in an error-filled first half, the Irish did their best. Sogge, who hadn't had a pass intercepted all season, had his first of three picked off and carried from the Trojan 25 to the 3, from where Hanratty rolled over. Suddenly it was 7–0, Notre Dame. And it stayed that way through the rest of the half as the Irish held Simpson to 41 yards in fourteen carries and stopped him on a couple of key third-down plays.

McKay and Goux roused them at intermission. Simpson was worked up. "I was disappointed in myself and determined to do better," he later recalled. They got a break at the beginning of the second half when Chuck Landolfi tried to field Tim Rossovich's short kickoff near the sidelines and Steve Swanson fell on the fumble for SC at the Irish 18. Notre Dame braced, but the ball went to Simpson again and again and he butted into the big guys again and again. He ran for 3 yards and for 11 yards. He was thrown for a 4-yard loss. He ran for 6 yards. He ran for another yard. On fourth down from the 1, Simpson took the ball and drove at the left side and dived over it, somersaulting through the maze of arms and legs into the end zone for the tying touchdown.

Notre Dame tried to come back, but Hanratty kept getting his passes picked off. One was returned 18 yards to the Irish 42 midway in the third quarter. After two plays gained 6 yards, Simpson took it on third and four and went 36 yards for his longest run of the season and a touchdown. Sogge took the snap and started left on the option play. He did not throw, and waited until he was about to be hit to pitch back to the trailer, Simpson, who took it and turned the corner with it. Tackle Hardy and defensive back Tom O'Leary rushed up to meet him, but O.J. accelerated and burst right between them into the open and streaked down the south sidelines alongside stands full of shocked Irish rooters, outdistancing his pursuers to reach the end zone and make it 14–7.

It was a remarkable run. Notre Dame aide Johnny Ray had been standing on the sidelines with a headset on in telephonic communication to the spotters upstairs, who had been telling him how to hold down Simpson, when Simpson shot past. "Oh, no," shouted Ray. "Oh, no . . . No . . . No . . . Oh, damn. . . . Damn!" The run seemed to break his spirit and his side's spirit.

In one blazing burst, Simpson had broken the game wide open.

After that, he kept cutting at them, driving at them, or circling around them, ripping them for a few yards here, a few more there. After a rushed Bleier caught a punt on the side of his foot and it went only 13 yards to the Notre Dame 41, SC was set up by a 17-yard run by Simpson for a short field goal by Aldridge that made it 17–7 late in the third session.

Early in the fourth quarter, Battle got the fifth interception from Hanratty and ran it back 36 yards to the Irish 17. Trying to make the tackle, Hanratty was knocked out and knocked out of the game. Simpson soon thrust 3 yards for his third touchdown that put the game out of reach, 24–7.

Coley O'Brien replaced Hanratty, but threw two more interceptions. Linebacker Young, an Irishman born in Dublin, but a Trojan on this day, had four of the seven SC picked off and he and Snow made twenty-six tackles between them to key an aroused defense that tied up the Irish offense. Simpson's runs contributed ball control. He got 109 yards in twenty-four runs in the second half. He wound up with 150 yards on thirty-eight carries.

At the gun, the saddened spectators in the stands had gone silent, but the Trojans went wild, the players picking up McKay on their shoulders and toting him off in triumph while the assistants danced with one another. The team trooped into its dressing room, roaring, "We're Number One!" which they were then. It took a long time for the tumult to quiet down a bit. Then a limp-looking McKay, sitting in a corner, was heard to say, "I haven't slept since last season's loss. I'll get a good night's sleep tonight." A worn-out seeming Simpson said, "I will, too," though he denied any exhaustion.

Ara Parseghian, the Notre Dame coach, said, "What can I say? We got beat. Bad. Simpson is outstanding. And they have an outstanding team." The Irish publicist, Roger Valdiserri, said, "Simpson's nickname shouldn't be 'Orange Juice.' It should be, 'Oh, Jesus.' As in 'Oh, Jesus,' there he goes again."

O.J. and the Trojans flew home to L.A. where a crowd of between two and three thousand supporters welcomed them, packing International Airport. They chanted, "We're Number One," over and over again, and when O.J. and many teammates got off the plane wearing green beanies purchased from hawkers outside the stadium, everyone cheered and laughed. Speaking briefly to the throng, McKay admitted, "This game has to be my biggest thrill."

Asked to compare this team with his 1962 championship team, McKay smiled and said, "They are very similar. Both of them were five and oh at this point."

So there they were, halfway to an undefeated season. But keeping pace was UCLA, which had edged past Tennessee and Penn State and routed Pitt, Washington State, and California and also was 5 and 0 and posed a threat to its crosstown rival's hopes for the national title, the conference crown, and the Rose Bowl berth. At midseason, matters in this sector's college football circles were steaming.

5 The Schlepper

At midseason of his first big-time season, the remarkable rookie O.J. Simpson was averaging thirty rushes a game, as well as running back kicks from time to time, running with passes from time to time, and throwing passes here and there. And it was a pace he would just about sustain through the remainder of that season, then actually increase noticeably the following season.

Melvin Durslag of the Los Angeles *Herald-Examiner* wrote a column in which, in search of a nickname for this new superstar he suggested "The Super Schlepper." In Jewish terminology, in Yiddish, Durslag explained, a schlep, the guy who schleps, the schlepper, is that patsy in every family who bears most of the burdens for most of the others, the poor slob who suffers so the others survive.

In football, at USC, Durslag noted, O.J. Simpson was the all-time, all American, undefeated heavyweight champion schlepper.

When some suggested McKay might be using Simpson too much, McKay shrugged and asked, "Why shouldn't we? The ball isn't heavy. Anyway, he can't complain. He doesn't belong to a union."

Simpson was being compared to Jimmy Brown. One

striking similarity surfaced following runs. As Brown used to do, Simpson would lie still, as though utterly exhausted, possibly even slain. He would rise with what appeared to be enormous effort. And he would walk back to the huddle with what appeared to be enormous effort. Slowly. Wearily. Or so it seemed. But just when you figured he was finished his number would be called again and he would run fast as though fresh, almost with reckless abandon. Often his early runs were only modestly productive. But usually he gained more and more as the games ground on and the tacklers tired.

It all made Durslag recall a story: When Carmen Basillio informed his onion-farmer father that he was going to be a boxer, the father said, "You gonna take a lot of lickings." Carmen said, "I know, Pop, but I'm gonna give a lot, too." Well, Carmen went on to become a champion and Simpson was on his way to that level, too. He was taking a pounding, but he was dealing out poundings and he was prevailing. Durslag recalled when Jim Brown's coach Paul Brown was accused of using Jim too much. "He'll soon get punch-drunk from getting hit so much," they said. Paul smiled and replied, "A lot of guys who hit him will get punch-drunk, too."

Durslag pointed out that Simpson's rest periods after being taken down and his leisurely returns to the huddle were fashioned after Brown's way of conserving energy. And Simpson went Brown one better. When taken with a tackle he could not break, O.J. would merely lean forward and fall, figuring that a man who had been carrying the ball as many as thirty-eight times in a game was "exposing himself to immense sadness if he wrestles with tacklers each time."

Instead of antagonizing tacklers, O.J. would then help them up and say something to them like "Nice hit," thus making them feel friendly instead of unfriendly. The next hit might not be quite so hard. They had no reason to try to finish off a friend. He seemed a sportsman and made it seem just a game. By the time it was over, he had beaten them.

Of course, all foes were pointing for him by halfway through his first season. Defenses were rigged to stop him. But he was hard to stop. He was a dandy and durable. McKay said, "He is much more like Gale Sayers that Jim Brown. At six-two and a hundred ninety-seven pounds, he is big, but not nearly as big as Brown. He doesn't collide with tacklers like a crashing runner does. He veers a lot and is moving away from the tackler when hit. He manages to avoid most of the impact and so is not punished severely. He's a smooth, gliding type of runner with a big upper body. He has thin legs, but a lot of strength above in his upper torso. And he is incredibly quick and fast. Being quick is one thing, fast another. Few runners are both. Simpson is both.

"One of the most impressive things to me is that in the five games he has played for me he has yet to make a mental mistake. He has never missed an audible, has yet to hit the wrong hole or mess up a play. For a youngster and a newcomer, this is remarkable. He has the right instincts, which may make him comparable to a Brown or Sayers before long."

Simpson himself said, "Yes, I copy Brown in the way I grab a rest by staying down an extra moment, get up slowly, and don't rush back to the huddle. I'm not trying to con anyone, but maybe it does lull the opposition into thinking I'm more tired than I really am. But I really am tired. You can't carry the ball thirty or more times a game and get hit as many times as I do and get brought down and have guys land on top of you without it taking something out of you. But, mostly, I feel it later. During games, I'm stirred up. I'm in shape, I'm strong and I seem to have a lot of stamina. Somehow, I keep going. I psych myself. I say to myself, 'C'mon, O.J., just one more.' And it's always there when I ask myself for it. I hustle. No one can say I'm not a worker. But jumping up and rushing back to the huddle would be a foolish waste of energy I'm going to need.

"I don't copy Brown or Sayers in the way I run. Oh, I've tried to in the past. But I try to play smart. I try to run smart. I might have picked up some things from them. I admire them enormously. I might give a guy a loose leg like Brown did. When the guy hits my leg, I let it go all soft. He relaxes and I make a muscle and yank it away and go on my way. Brown would let his free arm swing loosely on the tackler's side when he ran and when they went to put their arms around him he'd swing the arm hard and knock their arms aside. I try that sometimes. Sayers had moves I can't describe, but I've tried to imitate some. But mostly I've found you can't copy other runners too much because you can't outthink tacklers, you don't have time, you just have to get past them and you have to do it on instinct.

"My big advantages are my quickness, which enables me to get to a hole and through it quickly when it opens and I spot it, my moves, and my flat-out speed in the open field. I can cut sharper than most backs and I'm quicker and faster than most, especially those my size. I don't have the moves of a Sayers, but I have moves which sometimes surprise even me when I see them on film later. But I'm just learning. I learn some things every game now. Maybe small things, but they all help. I'm getting better. I think I have a long way to go. Getting a lot of opportunities helps me. It tires me, but I like it. I mean I wouldn't pile up nearly as much yardage if I wasn't running nearly as much. And I do seem to get most of my yardage late in games.

"I've surprised even myself by how well I've done," he admitted. "But I've never before had the blocking help I get on this team. I think this must be the greatest team in the country and that's our goal now, to prove it. We're rated tops now, but we have to hold on to it and there are some tough games ahead of us. I'm more concerned with our winning than me winning any individual honors. But the better year I have, the better year my team is apt to have. And if I can avoid injuries, this looks like some kind of year," he concluded.

He was giving such interviews several times every day. USC coach McKay and publicist Don Andersen tried to protect him from the pressure of the press and public, but he was so sensational and so in demand, and so agreeable to it that most of the national and local magazine and newspaper writers and television and radio broadcasters got to him and it was astonishing how well he handled it all.

He was twenty years old and supposedly unsophisticated and just getting schooled and really on the roaster for the first time and veterans were pumping questions at him and eyeing him closely and judging his responses carefully and often repeating these to the public not so carefully and yet he did not dodge the difficult questions, he gave honest answers, he smiled a lot and laughed easily and seemed sincere and seemed never to get flustered or annoyed.

You have to see it to understand how hard it is—the press coming at you in seemingly endless amounts, never letting you alone, often asking the same questions again and again and again—and it takes a superior personality of superior poise to take it in stride and do it right. O.J. did. He also spent hours signing autographs and appeared at as many clubs as he could.

Across town at UCLA, the Bruin football star Gary Beban was similarly splendid in his public and press relations, but the school's basketball star, Lew Alcindor, as he was known at the time, had retreated behind an iron curtain thrown around him there, and he was seldom available to anyone, and seldom agreeable or informative when he was out in the open, and the contrast between him and O.J. was striking. Some predicted O.J. was making life easier and happier for himself and would be more at ease with life later and more popular with his way than Lew would be with his way and this is exactly how it turned out. Years later, Simpson seems free, while Kareem Jabbar, as Alcindor now is known, seems still hunted and often in hiding.

At the time, Simpson smiled and said, "Oh, it's all a plot, you know. Someday it may make me a lot of money. I'm planning on the pros and if I'm popular, it will help." But the writer pressed him, pointing out it would be emotionally impossible for him to remain on an even keel through constant confrontations with the press and public if it wasn't a natural part of his nature. O.J. nodded his head and admitted, "It's me. It comes easy because it's me. I'm no saint. I got a lot of hell in me. But not much hatred. I like people. I'm easygoing by nature. I've always tried to be an agreeable guy. And I enjoy the spotlight. I like being a celebrity. It's fun to stand out. I guess some guys don't like it. I do."

Dutch Elston pointed out that the night he reminded O.J. he would have to make a speech when he was honored as his junior college league's Player of the Year, O.J. just smiled and said, "I'm all set, Coach." Elston recalls, "The award was given in honor of a fellow named McFadden, who used to be athletic director of San Mateo College. There were a lot of speakers on the program, but O.J. was the only one who spoke about Mr. McFadden and the only one who acknowledged McFadden's widow was in the audience. No one told him to. A nineteen-year-old kid and he just seemed to know that was the thing to do. And a lot older people didn't know it."

At twenty, at USC, Simpson was making a similar impression. In the Los Angeles *Times*, this was written: "He has handled the football challenges in remarkable fashion. But what he has done with the off-the-field pressures may be even more impressive. The demands on his time are incredible. Everybody wants him—writers, broadcasters, clubs, conventions, alumni, fans, kids. And he accommodates most of them.

It is almost inevitable that he will become one of the highest-paid professional athletes in history. But there is a basic decency and honesty about him that transcends the monetary considerations. He is a football player of once-in-a-lifetime talent, but he also is an intelligent, sensitive young man."

Both aspects of him were being thoroughly tested.

6 The Big Tests

Against the University of Washington Huskies in Seattle, O.J. Simpson broke a big one—an 86-yard scoring run. On first down from his own 10, Simpson ran for 4. On second down, he ran for 86. He faked right, then cut back over left guard where Mike Taylor and Steve Lehmer had opened a hole. As Simpson shot through, Ron Yary brushed aside a linebacker and Jim Lawrence cut down a defensive back. Simpson burst through the bunch, came into the clear at the 30, and sprinted the final 70 yards before being caught from behind.

The field had been rained soft and slippery and it was a stunning run, which silenced a record crowd of 58,000 rooters for awhile. They had hoped the slow field would slow Simpson. For awhile after that, it did. The Huskies marched 80 yards to a field goal that cut their deficit to 7–3 at halftime. And McCullouch's fumble of the opening kickoff of the second half set up another field goal that sliced the score to 7–6 early in the third quarter.

This was a good Washington team, which had not been scored on in the second half all season. At this point, an upset seemed possible and the pressure piled up on the Trojans. But Simpson, although he limped off with leg cramps at one time, returned and kept slashing.

Late in the quarter, he helped get going a short drive to the Washington 10 from where he scored early in the last quarter. He had been told the left end tended to pinch in to help out on his inside drives and he might be able to circle around him. O.J. took the handoff, made a move inside left as the end darted in, then turned outside, turned the corner beyond the end's desperate dive, and simply outran a defensive back into the end zone. Now, USC led, 14–6.

On the next series, the Washington center snapped the ball back over his punter's head and outside of the end zone for a safety that made it 16–6. Then, after USC failed to move and punted, the Washington receiver fumbled the punt on his 15 and McCullouch fell on it. The Trojans lost ground on three plays, but on fourth down they gave the ball to Simpson, who circled to one side, reversed his field to the other side, eluded tackler after tackler, spotted McCullouch open in the end zone, and pitched a 17-yard strike to him. That made it 23–6 and what had been a hard game suddenly seemed easy. It was Simpson's fifth pass of the season and third touchdown completion. He had also gained 235 yards on thirty rushes. His average run of 7.8 yards was to be the highest of his college career.

Afterwards, O.J. sat in the dressing room with tiny blades of grass, which he was too weary to brush off stuck all over his forehead. His teammates were teasing him. "What were the stats on O.J. today?" one asked. "How long was that long run?" another asked. "How many yards did he gain?" a third yelled. It was a splendid scene of success in which the star was being saluted by his supporting cast. O.J. just grinned.

Grinning at his grin, McCullouch said, "He is the star, but we have other starry guys on this cast and if he was any different than he is it would be easy to envy him or be jealous of him or look to put him down, but he doesn't act like a star. He acts like just one of the guys, he has a hard job to do and he does it and we respect him for the way he does it and like him for the way he is. It's tough for a top player to see all the news guys around him all the time, but we see he rates it and we know he doesn't ask for it and he spreads the credit around. He's not humble. He knows he's good. But he's grateful for the help he gets. He's modest. He's quite a man."

Simpson was saying, "I get the leg cramps all the time. Maybe from running so much. Or getting hit so much. But they pass. I thought I was running better than I had at any time this year. But it may have gone to my head. I made more running mistakes than I have in any game. I made mistakes. I fumbled the ball. We took a long time breaking the ballgame open and I was partly responsible. After the long one, I started to gamble on another instead of running right and letting come what comes."

Assistant coach Dave Levy said, "When he makes an error, he doesn't pout. He just comes right back. I've seen backs have more spectacular games and backs have fewer mistakes, but Simpson does it when it counts, baby."

McKay stood with his back to a wall, cornered by the press, and he said, "I guess he was due to make a mistake or two, but he didn't make many, and he made the big runs and big yardage, as usual. We took awhile doing it, but we won. But I was a bit disappointed at the finish."

"Why?" a writer asked.

"The team didn't carry me off the field," McKay said.

"What about O.J.'s leg cramps?"

"He has a tendency to get them when he carries the ball fifty times," McKay said.

"Did you know he left the game only sixteen yards short of C.R. Roberts' one-game school record for rushing yardage?"

"No."

"There was still time left for him to run some more. If you'd known, would have left him in the game?" a writer asked.

"No," McKay said. "No, I wouldn't have."

He had worked him until the game was won and then the coach had removed his star runner for fear of having him hurt when he was no longer needed. His exertions had slimmed the slender runner 11 pounds to 193, but he said, "I'm enjoying it. It makes you feel like you're always in the game. It helps your concentration. It helps make you a better runner. I knew I'd be running more in college than I did in junior college, but I had no idea I'd run this much. But I can handle it."

He had gained 987 yards in six games. He was about to become only the second Trojan to run for more than 1,000 yards in a season, he was ahead of the pace Mike Garrett set when he set the school record of 1,440 yards in one year, and he was even ahead of the pace set by Fred Wendt of Texas Mines when he set the one-season NCAA record of 1,570 yards in 1948. Simpson was averaging more than 5 yards a carry and was being heralded for the Heisman Trophy, along with Gary Beban of UCLA. The Bruins had slipped past Stanford, 21–16, to keep pace with the Trojans and now were the number-two team in the nation, trailing only number-one USC.

The Big Game seemed to be getting bigger by the week. Both teams were looking forward to it.

It is possible UCLA was looking too far forward. The next week, the Bruins were tied by a rugged Oregon State team, 16–16. At the same time, USC may have been a bit guilty, too. They looked bad in beating a bad Oregon team 28–6 at the Coliseum. And though the Trojans won, while the Bruins were tied, the Trojans emerged just as dejected because they came out of the contest with O.J. injured.

He went into the game averaging 165 yards a game and came out averaging 150 yards a game after being held to 63 yards in twenty-three carries in this game by a grudging Oregon defense as long as he lasted. He might have picked up the pace because he might have wound up with forty carries if he had not been eliminated early in the second half.

Going up the middle, he was stopped for no gain by middle guard George Daimes. "My foot got turned the wrong way and someone fell on it," Simpson recalled later. It was his right foot and the arch was sprained severely and he had to be helped off the field and then he sat on the bench with an ice pack on his foot and watched Steve Grady replace him and run for 108 yards in eighteen carries as USC pulled away.

Afterwards, in the dressing room, Simpson said, "Grady was super. That's why this is a super team. Because we have super players behind our regulars. I got to give Oregon credit. They were stopping me. Could they have continued to do it? I don't know. As long as they had to, they did it. But we won, which is what counts. And I don't think my foot is hurt too bad. I'm sure I'll be ready for the California game next week. I've never missed any games in my career and I don't want to start now."

But that night the foot swelled up severely and began to hurt a lot. Doctors examined it and wrapped the sprain tightly and put the player on crutches and said he'd have to stay off the foot indefinitely.

The next day O.J. said, "Yesterday the foot throbbed all the time, but today it only hurts when I put weight on it. The doctors say I'll be out two weeks. That means I'll miss the Cal game unless there's a miracle. Will I be ready for the Oregon State game? I hope so. The UCLA game? I hope so. We're down to the nitty-gritty now and I hate like heck to miss any of it."

He sat in his apartment with his foot hiked up on a bench and his wife applying an ice bag to the bandaged ankle. He held his crutches in his lap, running his hands over them restlessly, looking at his foot. He lapsed into silence, his face somber as he stared at his foot.

Coach McKay said, "He got us this far. Now we'll just have to go on awhile without him." And at Berkeley, the Trojans trimmed a mediocre California club, 31–12 without him. And at Corvallis, the Trojans got him back, but without practice.

Bravely, he returned. He limped onto the field, which was wet and muddy from a typical Northwest torrent. And then he ran his heart out, and McKay did not take it easy on him. He rushed thirty-three times for 188 yards in one of the most stunning shows an injured player ever has put on, but he could not make it into the end zone, the SC attack stalled again and again, mired in the mud, and a field goal upset them 3–0, ending their hopes of going undefeated. UCLA walloped Washington, 48–0, and replaced USC as the number-one-rated team in the nation.

So it came down to *The Biggest Game*, not only the usual intense battle for the city crown which comes in good years and bad, but a battle that went beyond the boundaries of this area in interest: The national title, the conference crown, and the Rose Bowl berth hung in the balance. With the Simpson-Beban battle for the Heisman Trophy and the McKay-Prothro duel for coaching laurels as arresting sidelights. The Trojans emerged from the Oregon State debacle deeply disappointed and determined to end UCLA's run of two straight intracity triumphs and reclaim the honors it had held in its hands most of the long, difficult campaign.

More than 90,000 fans filled the Coliseum and millions more tuned in to national television on this mid-November southern California-sunny Saturday afternoon. Starting fast, Beban passed the Bruins into position that blocked for Greg Jones' 12-yard run which put UCLA in front. But then a Beban pass was intercepted by Pat Cashman and returned 55 yards to tie it. And then McCullouch covered 65 yards on a run and a pass and Simpson shook off six tacklers in a short but stunning 13-yard scamper to a 14–7 intermission lead.

Before the game, Marv Goux had held up a picture of John McKay staring at the ground after the previous year's loss to UCLA and told the team they had to win this one for this man who had put up with so much from them and put so much into them. They had to win it for themselves, the seniors, too, because they had lost two to this team and if they lost this one they would leave without ever even once having won this game and he had whipped them into the frenzy that took them to the halftime lead.

And now, at intermission, with the lead, McKay said they had it but they could let it get away from them and that they'd probably have to play a better second half than they had a first half it they were to be in the lead at the end and the walk from the field at the finish would either be the shortest or longest of their lives.

And they went out and ran right into an inspired bunch of Bruins. Beban threw 47 yards to George Farmer for the tying touchdown. And then he threw and threw and threw finally 20 yards to Dave Nuttall for the lead. But all this time, big Bill Hayhoe and other Trojans had risen up to block two field-goal tries and one extra-point try by Zeno Andrusyshyn and the Bruins remained vulnerable at 20–14.

And in that madness that was in this emotionally charged saucer, in the descending darkness, O.J. Simpson, ignoring his seriously sore foot, ran the kickoff back from his goal line to the 34, and then on third down from the 36, after Toby Page, in for Sogge, checked off a pass play at the line of scrimmage and called for what had worked for his side all season, a run by Simpson, O.J. hurried through a hole, reversed his field, broke tackles, broke free, and sprinted to the historic touchdown that with Rikki Aldridge's conversion settled the issue, 21–20.

It was about as good as a game could be, leaving the USC rooters roaring and the UCLA supporters weeping and all who saw it limp at the finish and the USC team whooping and hollering happily in their dressing room and the UCLA team sitting silently in sadness in their quarters. And the stars came together afterward; Simpson, who had run thirty times for 177 yards and two touchdowns, and Beban, who had passed twenty-four times for 301 yards and two touchdowns, and they spoke softly and respectively to one another and then went on their ways; Simpson, voted the Back of the Game, to the Rose Bowl, and Beban, voted the Player of the Year, to the Heisman Trophy award ceremonies.

Most felt Simpson would have won if he had been a senior, but he conducted himself with class and refused to complain. He said, "They voted the man the honor, so that is it. I am disappointed for myself, but I am a fan of his and he is marvelous."

There is a long wait and a big buildup to the Rose Bowl. The Southern California Trojans spent six weeks practicing to take on the Indiana University Fighting Hoosiers, surprised survivor of the Big Ten tournament. John Pont had been brought in as the

THE BIG TESTS

latest in a long line of coaches trying to elevate the Cream and Crimson from the lower ranks of the conference's football forces and with a young and gambling group, headed by John Isenbarger and Harry Gonso, the Boys from Bloomington had pulled off a series of upsets to land in Pasadena for the first time.

They had made miracles throughout the 1967 season, but ran out of them on the first day of 1968. Before a record crowd of 102,996 fans squeezed into this ancient, sprawling saucer, Simpson led Southern Cal to a spare but convincing 14–3 New Year's Day triumph.

On their first series, USC marched to 7–0. Simpson carried the ball six times in the thirteen plays for 41 of the 86 yards covered and he made the last two from third down when there was no hole and he leaped and cannonballed over the pile, landing just past the goal line.

On the second series, after Indiana fumbled the ball away on its own 27, SC decoyed Simpson seven straight plays and wound up fumbling the ball back before it could increase its edge.

The Trojans returned to Simpson, but penalties nullified four of his gains including a 28-yard run to the Hoosier 13 in the second quarter and the Trojans could not find the scoring touch.

Late in the half, Gonso made a fine return of a punt to set up a field goal which sliced SC's lead to 7–3 at intermission.

In the third period, a poor punt gave the Trojans field position on the Hoosier 45 and they moved the ball in on a pass by Sogge and three runs by Simpson. The last run by Simpson was only 8 yards long, but he made it a masterpiece, as he often did with short but stirring scoring romps.

Sogge sprung a trap on third and four, faking a dropback to pass, drawing the rushers in, then handing off to Simpson, who shot inside of them. Two Hoosiers had angles on him, but he got through so fast as they closed in on him that they wound up tackling each other a split second after he had departed. His leg went loose like limp spaghetti and two tacklers slipped off. He shifted and raced into the end zone and it was 14–3.

It ended that way. The Hoosiers fought furiously and stopped further scoring thrusts, but could not score themselves. Simpson wound up with 128 yards on twenty-five carries and was voted Player of the Game. Writing in *The Sporting News*, Bob Oates later observed, "Seldom in a football game has one halfback so clearly been the difference."

Losing coach Pont agreed. He said later, "USC was the best team we played this season because of Simpson. If Simpson had been on any other team we met this season, that would have been the best team we played. They were good and their defense stopped us, but he beat us." He sat on a desk in the losers' quiet room and fussed with the crease on his trousers and said, "He is some player."

McKay said, "O.J. was great as usual, but this was a team triumph." He was flushed with happiness and relief and he had to shout to be heard over the joyous yells of his victorious team in their quarters. The players had protected their number-one ranking and the mythical national crown and this tenth victory in eleven starts completed an outstanding campaign.

Simpson sat tired and smiling broadly and asked, "Does this mean I don't have to carry the ball thirty times on Saturday?" All agreed it meant at least that. He said, "I'm tired, but it's been a great season, a great season for me and a greater season for the team. I'm not trying to be modest when I ask you to give the other guys credit. No runner runs anywhere without holes to run through and blockers to help him along. I did more than my share maybe, but everyone did all they could and there are some tremendous players on this team. It wouldn't matter what we scored if the defense didn't hold them to less."

He rubbed a grass stain off his soiled skin, grinned and said, "This has to be the greatest. Ol' O.J. from Potrero Hill in the Rose Bowl . . . and a winner!" SC finished 10–0–1, national kings, having outscored their foes, 258–87.

After he had showered and changed he went out into the night and stood for a long time smiling and accepting congratulations and signing autographs for all the youngsters who had waited until the last scrap of paper had his special "Oh Jay Simpson" scrawled on it.

At twenty, he had put together an almost incomparable campaign. He had rushed the ball 291 times for 1543 yards and thirteen touchdowns. Missing one game had made him miss the national rushing record by 27 yards. He averaged twenty-nine carries a game and more than 5 yards a carry through ten games. He had become his school's single-season rushing leader, surpassing the 267 carries and 1,440 yards gained by

Mike Garrett in his senior season when he won the Heisman Trophy. Simpson had been second in his Heisman balloting, but he had made every single All-American team selected. And he was voted Player of the Year ahead of Beban by the Associated Press and United Press International.

He eased off some. He became a full-time student, improving his grades noticeably. He said, "This is a great school. I'm lucky to be here. I have to take advantage of it." He and Marguerite lived quietly. He said, "You sure have a lot of adjustments to make when you get married, but we're making them." She smiled and said, "I'm making them." She went on working as a library clerk at Science Hall and in the spring she became pregnant and they looked forward to the birth of their first child late in the year. He said, "I'd like to have a son, but my sister's little girls are something, too." He ran track. And the school year ended.

He spent most of the summer near the campus and he spent a lot of time working with youngsters. He said, "I remember some of those people who worked with me when I was coming up. Lots of guys come out of high school and they're not quite developed. I want to try to help people like that." He was hailed as a hero wherever he went, but he moved modestly. His mother said, "Kids always have surrounded him and worshipped him. And he always has had the time for them."

Asked about pro ball and a possible fat pact, he smiled and shrugged and tried to set it aside. "That's a way off. I got a whole year of college yet to go." He hunched over a little and looked down and said, "The injury I got scared me some. I know I'd been getting away lucky. I know one 'pop' and it can all go. But you can't let it get to you. You got to forget it and go all-out."

He said, "I got tired sometimes last season. More than I'd let on. And my legs would cramp up. And I couldn't sleep after games. It's not easy, you know. But I can't complain. It all went too good to gripe. Sure I look forward to playing pro. That's the top isn't it? And to making some money, I never had any, you know. But I got a big year to get through first."

He looked up and his face went wistful and he said, "I suppose the pressure will be worse than ever now. It's gonna' be hard to top what we done, but everyone's gonna' be expecting it. Aw, hell, I guess it'll be all right. I don't suppose I can work any harder or get hit any harder."

7 Harder and Harder

On the eve of the new season, his senior season, O.J. Simpson said, "I want the Heisman Trophy. I'd be lying if I said I didn't. I want to become a pro star and I'd like a good contract. But, first things first. Guys win the Heisman Trophy every year. One every year, anyway. Guys are drafted into the pros every year. But guys don't have a chance to play on a team which wins two straight national championships every year. We do. SC won the title last year and can win it this year. That's my big goal right now—to help any way I can.

"The Heisman Trophy probably will be between Leroy Keyes and me. I finished second and he finished third in the voting last season. We were juniors. Gary Beban, a senior, won it. I think the best man should win it. I think juniors have a hard time winning it and I don't think it should matter. A man's best year may be his junior year. I think Beban's best years were his sophomore and junior years. I may never have another year like my junior year. But that's the way it is and now we're seniors and we both want it.

"A lot may depend on how our teams do. I've only seen Leroy play once—in the Rose Bowl against USC after the 1966 season—but I know he does real well. At six-three, he's a little taller than I am. He's not quite as fast, but he's clever. When he runs, he sort of floats. He knows how to follow his blockers real well. And he's real cool, too. He has a smile on his face all the time, even when he's knocking into people.

"He's very versatile. He's not only a running back, but an outstanding defensive back. He's a good receiver. And he kicks off and place-kicks, too. I don't do all those things. I have done most of them. I could do most of them. But not carrying the ball thirty times a game. Carrying the ball as much as I did last year, I don't think I could have played on defense, too. You might say I felt a bit beat most of the time. Keyes doesn't carry the ball nearly as much as I do. But he does the other things.

"He's a good guy. I keep running into him at banquets. I'm almost rooting for him.

"While we're watching each other, Terry Hanratty of Notre Dame might beat us out. Five of the last six years they've given the award to quarterbacks, which is what Hanratty is—one of the best on one of the best teams. Another thing against me may be that two of the last three years the award has gone to a West Coast guy—first Mike Garrett of USC, then Gary Beban of UCLA. The voters may play a regional game. They may not want to give it to another USC guy. They may not want to give it to another West Coast guy.

"I'll just have to do my best. The funny thing is, the better I do, the worse the pro team that'll get to draft me. They start at the bottom and work up. It seems somehow unfair. I'd like to be drafted by an NFL team. I guess they're merging, but the NFL and AFL still seem like two different leagues to me. I've been an

NFL guy all my life. I watched the 49ers in San Francisco most of my life and I've been watching the Rams in L.A. since I got here and I'd love to be taken by one of those teams.

"I'm a Californian. I'd like to play pro in my home state. It seems like a fellow should have a choice. If I did go to an AFL team, I'd like to be on the first one to win the Super Bowl. One thing, I'd hate to land on a loser—one of those expansion teams or a bad team. It's selfish, sure, but if you do, your first deal better be a good one because you may never get as good a chance again. Running behind a weak line you can't expect to have big years statistically.

"Well, it's something I'll just have to deal with when the time comes. Right now it's time to start the new season at SC. My last season and it seems like I just got here, which is what is different when you go to junior college first. We lost a lot of our top players to graduation. We have a lot of top players to move up, but they're much more inexperienced than the other players were. If we can develop the same attitude we had last year in the first few games, we'll be all right. We got to thinking no one could beat us. Confidence carries you a long way.

"I'm a lot more confident than I was going into last season. I always had confidence in myself but I hadn't done it in real college competition before and now I have and it makes a difference in my feelings. I proved myself to myself as much as to anyone else. But I can't play on last year. That's gone. That's then. This is now. It's a whole new deal. Except for the experience I got and the improvements I made, last season can't help me this season. All my stats and clippings and honors won't gain me one yard. I can't be complacent or cocky. I got to go out and do it. We got to go out and do it."

He walked out into the September sunshine. He walked loose and easy. In civvies, dressed casually in sports clothes, he does not seem as big as he is. He was back to his playing weight of 204 pounds now, but he carries his weight well. He seems slender. He walks with an easy gait. He is a handsome young man. His head is a little large for his body, but he has good features and a fast, pleasant smile. He has a sincere manner and a winning personality. He was twenty-one now and he was a man.

Back in his apartment, on his record player, a record was spinning and the Impressions were singing, "We're moving up. Lord have mercy. We're a winner...."

The Southern Cal football team had been rebuilt. There were key returnees and a lot of outstanding but unproven young players moving into regular roles. The defense was anchored by end Jimmy Gunn, tackles Al Cowlings and Tony Terry, linebacker Jim Snow, and defensive backs Mike Battle and Gerry Shaw. The offensive line had been constructed around center Dick Allmon, guard Fred Khasigian, tackles Sid Smith and Jack O'Malley, and tight-end Bob Klien. Steve Sogge had settled in at quarterback. His wide receivers were Jim Lawrence, Bob Chandler, and Sam Dickerson. His runners were Dan Scott and O.J. Simpson.

The season opened in Minneapolis, where the Trojans took on the Big Ten's Minnesota Golden Gophers on a drizzly, wet September Saturday afternoon. Minnesota was rated a tough test for the defending national champions and a crowd of 60,000 filled the stadium. And the hosts turned out to be tough. But Simpson turned out to be tougher. On a field covered with high, slippery grass, he carried the ball a career high thirty-nine times for a career high 236 yards and all four of his team's touchdowns. He also caught six passes for 57 yards and ran back kicks for 72 yards, giving him a total offense of 365 yards. It took two or three, sometimes four or five tacklers to stop him. At the end, as usual, it was almost impossible to stop him.

Southern Cal had to come from 10 points behind to win with a late rally. This was partly Simpson's own fault. He fumbled twice and one gave Minnesota a touchdown and the other took one away from USC. After his first fumble on his own 15, the Gophers moved right in to go up to 7–0. By the end of the first period, a field goal had made it 10–0 and Minnesota's fans were roaring and SC seemed in trouble.

In the second quarter, Simpson ran 36 yards to SC's first touchdown. He cut to his left, broke two tackles, feinted out two other tacklers, and simply outraced the secondary into the end zone. Later he and Sogge led a drive that was climaxed when O.J. jumped over from 1 yard out to put the Trojans in front, 13–10. An exchange of field goals made it 16–13.

Minnesota's George Kemp took a kickoff and arched a lateral pass far to his right to John Wintermute, who darted 83 yards to a 20–16 Minnesota lead with little more than seven minutes remaining.

Simpson went to work. He carried the ball on all six plays of a forceful 45-yard march that put the Trojans back in front, 20–16. The score came on a 3-yard thrust. Then he carried the ball five times in six plays of a 37-yard drive to the 7-yard run that sewed it up at 29–20.

Later, Minnesota's coach Murry Warmath said, "They said he was the greatest, but he's better than that." USC coach McKay observed, "It's obvious he's much improved this season. I could live without his fumbles, but he more than makes up for them."

Simpson said, "My fumbles mostly seem to come when I'm struggling for an extra yard. I don't like them at all, but I guess when you carry the ball thirty to forty times a game they're gonna happen sometimes. You keep getting hit hard by guys who often are trying to hit the ball, too, or steal it, and you can't always keep control of it. You try to forget the fumbles. If you worry too much about protecting the ball, you can't run free. And I want to run free."

He seemed especially tired although this was only the first game of the season. His body had bruises on it. He insisted, "I don't mind running the ball this much. If you don't run, you have to fake or block. Faking is tiring and blocking is dangerous and running is more fun than either." But he admitted, "I feel sort of sore. I took a lot of punishment out there. I just shook it off and kept going. And the things which weren't working for me earlier began to work."

McKay said, "He always looks like an average guy early in the games, but he's far from average, which he proves as the games go on. I'm criticized for using him so much, but the more I use him the better he does, so I may use him even more in the future. I know he takes punishment, but he seems equal to it. We'll try to take it easy on him in practice. We'll try to save him for Saturdays."

So sore he didn't practice all week, Simpson went back to work on Saturday in Evanston, Illinois, where the Trojans took on Northwestern, another Big Ten team.

O.J. wasn't used as much as the week before. He only was given the ball thirty-four times. He gained 189 yards and scored three touchdowns on runs of 5, 11, and 15 yards. After the Wildcats closed to within 17–7 in the last period and the nearly 50,000 Chicago-area rooters were rooting their team on, O.J. took over. Four Simpson runs and a penalty covered 50 yards and sewed up the contest with sixty seconds left, 24–7.

Afterwards, Northwestern mentor Alex Agase said, "We did all we could. I don't know what can stop him. He sees daylight and runs to it. He's so quick and fast he's hard to catch and so strong he's hard to stop even if you catch him. If you took half your team to defense him, the other SC players would offense you to death, and I'm not sure he can be defensed, anyway."

McKay admitted. "I almost didn't play him. It wasn't a matter of not practicing him hard. It was a matter of him being to bruised-up to practice. I told him to tell me if he was ready and the last minute he said he was ready."

Simpson said, "I didn't feel ready until Friday. Coach said to let him know before the game. I told him I was OK before the game. I wasn't as quick and strong as I have been, but I guess I was OK. I had it when I needed it. And we won, which is all that matters. I'm sort of sore again now."

Wearily, he arose, stripped, and showered, trying to steam the soreness out of his tired body. He dressed in his fancy duds and went outside. It took him twenty minutes to get 50 yards from the locker room to the team bus because the fans surrounded him and he signed autographs for them.

Now, instead of "Oh Jay Simpson," he was signing simply, "O.J. Simpson," because it was shorter and he would do anything to save his strength some. Anything except not sign autographs. "I used to be a kid collecting autographs," he said. "I know what a star's name on a scrap of paper means to a kid."

He grinned, "It's funny. The adults always apologize and say they want the autograph for their kids. Don't adults ever want autographs?"

In Minneapolis and Chicago, the writers had gotten to him. He was the big story, the hot player. But Leroy Keyes had led Purdue to a 37–22 upset of Notre Dame and, especially in Chicago, everyone was wondering if Keyes could win the Heisman Trophy from Simpson. The season had just started, but the pressure was on Simpson, the player, and the Trojans, the team, already.

With his team, O.J. flew back to Los Angeles and his apartment, where the phone seemed to ring all the time. This newspaper columnist wanted to do a piece on him and that magazine writer was coming in from New York with a photographer for a spread. Every time he turned around, a microphone was being thrust in his face. He never seemed to have any real amount of free time for himself and his family.

Privately he confided, "It's starting to get to me. I thought I'd get used to it and it would get easier, but it's getting harder, instead. I don't feel real. It's like I'm a cardboard cutout and everyone wants to tear off a piece of me for themselves. It's taking all the fun out of it." But, publicly, he never let on.

The first Saturday night in October the University of Miami team came to town. More than 70,000 convened in the Coliseum to see Simpson and his side do their stuff. He was given the ball thirty-eight times and carried it 163 yards. He caught a couple of passes. He scored two touchdowns on short runs. His longest run was 30 yards. In his thirteenth varsity game he passed Orv Mohler's second-best-ever Trojan rushing total of 2,028 yards, collected in three years. Sogge and sub Mike Holmgren threw scoring passes to Lawrence and Chandler and SC coasted in, 28–3.

Now, however, the Trojans faced their sternest test yet. They had to go to Palo Alto to take on a Stanford team with an unusually good collection of talent and a sensational sophmore quarterback, Jim Plunkett. The undefeated Indians had a super-receiver in Gene Washington and a lethal linebacker in Don Parish. The Indians had lost ten straight to the Trojans and coach John Ralston had his forces fired up.

A tremendous turnout of 81,000 filled the big campus bowl to overflowing. The general feeling was that the winner would win the conference crown and the Rose Bowl bid. Although also undefeated, the defending national champion SC team was rated only second in the country, behind Purdue, and needed to keep winning to keep pace. Both sides were sky-high by game time and the tension in the arena was terrific.

Stanford took it right to SC, hitting hard and forcing three fumbles from Simpson. After Ron Ayala place-kicked SC to a 3–0 edge, Bubba Brown broke loose on a 51-yard run to put Stanford up, 7–3. Simpson sparked a drive that was finished off by his short run to put SC back on top, 10–7. But Steve Horowitz kicked a 38-yard field goal to send the struggle to intermission all even at 10–10.

In the third quarter, Plunkett passed 27 yards to Jack Lasater to put Stanford in front, 17–10. After SC failed, Stanford took over again and Plunkett passed again, but Shaw picked this one off and was brought down on the Stanford 46. On the first play, Simpson spurted for a touchdown that tied it, 17–17.

O.J. rolled around right end. Tackle O'Malley led him and flattened a cornerback and Simpson cut inside and was on his way 46 fast yards. "I found a little funnel to run into and then I cut it up," Simpson said later.

The great crowd was going wild over the great game.

Plunkett took his team right back to the lead, driving them deep, then running himself 10 yards to the tally that made it 24–17. Late in the third quarter, Sogge threw from the SC 48 to the Stanford 15, where Lawrence caught the ball and carried it to the 4 before being downed. Then O.J. made a fantastic 4-yard run to tie it again, 24–24.

Simpson struck over guard. A trio of Stanford defenders rose up and hit him so hard they knocked him off his feet and into the air. He squirmed, landed on his feet, maintained his balance, pushed off again, and ran right through three tackles, breaking them, and reached the end zone to even the contest.

The final quarter was fierce, with the two sides struggling for an edge. Finally, a series of short runs by Simpson took his team to the Stanford 22. Then he took the ball, started off tackle, saw no hole, reversed his field, started around the other end, spotted Scott open inside the 10 and threw to him. Scott caught it and went down at the 8 with a first down in his hands.

Stanford rose up and threw SC back 17 yards over three downs. On fourth down, Ayala moved in and place-kicked a 34-yard field goal that settled the issue, 27–24, leaving the home fans disillusioned. The Trojans ran off in triumph, the top team in the nation, Purdue having been upset by Ohio State.

Plunkett had passed for 247 yards and one touchdown. Simpson had run a career-high forty-seven times for a career-high 220 yards and three touchdowns. After being "held" to 77 yards in the first half, O.J. had fought free for 143 yards in the second half. He had been run so much the day didn't seem far off when he simply would get the ball on every play.

Stanford linebacker Don Parish said, "We contained him for a half, but then we got tired and he just got stronger."

Ralston said, "Simpson was sensational." McKay said, "Plunkett was magnificent." Plunkett said, "Simpson is simply super." Simpson said, "That Plunkett is something else. He's going to be great, if he's not already."

Plunkett, too, would win the Heisman Trophy in time, of course.

Simpson sat by his locker rubbing a left leg so sore he had missed a couple of days of practice again the preceding week. Entering the dressing room through a mob of fans, he had smiled and said, "When I come out, I'll get all of you, OK?" Now he showered and dressed and went out and stood there and got all of them. "O.J. Simpson" by "O.J. Simpson," scrawled signature by scrawled signature, until night was near and the air grew cold.

Next was Washington, in from Seattle in mid-October with one of Jim Owens' weakest teams. More than 60,000 came to the Coliseum to see they supposed a one-sided game. It turned out to be a defensive duel. And a dramatic one. The only score of the first half came on a 1-yard plunge by Simpson which gave SC a slim 7–0 intermission lead. And in the third period an interception off Sogge put the Huskies in close and they scored to tie it, 7–7.

Then, in the final period, Simpson's second fumble gave Washington the ball again in close, on the SC 25, and the Huskies hammered it to the 1 and seemed about to take the lead and perhaps the game. However, four tries later, the Huskies were still on the 1. A magnificent goal-line stand by the Trojans was climaxed when quarterback Tom Manke on a fourth-down keeper was hit by Al Cowlings, then Bubba Scott, then nine more Trojans.

Inspired, the Trojans took over the ball in terrible position, on their own 1, and proceeded to march a school-record 99 yards to the winning touchdown.

Anxious to atone for his almost fatal fumble, Simpson rushed seven times for 57 yards during the drive, slicing through the line and cutting back across the field 9 yards the last time to the touchdown that made it 14–7, the final score.

During this drive, Simpson ran with incredible power. Usually he had a straight-up-and-down posture when he ran. Sometimes when he bent over a bit he seemed to run and hit harder. In this march he hunched over a little and just tore through the opposition. In the end, he had run thirty-three times for 172 yards. This brought him to 191 carries for 980 yards and he was only at half-season. And he had scored fourteen of his team's sixteen touchdowns.

Washington's Owens sat as though stunned and said, "We went in twenty points underdogs but we should have come out seven points on top. As the game went on, I thought we'd win. We had great desire. In some ways we outplayed them. But we didn't stop Simpson. We stopped him for awhile, but you can only stop him so long. He's tremendous. He's their offense. He's their team. They have great players, but he makes them a great team. With him they can play poor or be outplayed and win. His only weakness is fumbles. He more than makes up for a few of those."

With this game, Simpson surpassed the 2,500-yard-mark in college career rushing. Yet he was only midway in his second season. He was worn out and relieved to be reminded SC had a week off before entering the second half of its season. His long fingers rubbing his slender legs, he sat on his stool too tired to move right away and said, "I welcome the break. I need it. We need it. It's nice to be undefeated, but when you are it sometimes seems every game is a crucial. They're all shooting for you when you're Number One and even a weak one can worry you. It's hard to be up every game and any time you're flat is a game you can be beat. The national title? The Rose Bowl? The Heisman Trophy? Sure, I want those things. That's why I'm bending my back. But there's a long road to go yet."

8 Concluding a Career

While O.J. Simpson entered the last half of his last season in quest of individual and team laurels, a number of pro teams entered the last part of their campaigns in quest of O.J. Simpson. It was a race for losers, with Buffalo, Philadelphia, and a few others in the running for the worst records, which would give them the best draft choice of the graduating collegians. Not that these teams were throwing games. They were able to lose legitimately. Complete with the consolation that the one that lost the most would get the player who was wanted the most—Simpson, the super-runner.

The press in those cities that were out of contention for laurels in their races and thus in contention for the plum publicized the situation excessively. Headlines like EAGLES LOSE, MOVE A STEP CLOSER TO SIMPSON were embarrassing. It was almost certain O.J. would go to a bad team. Some good teams, including the Los Angeles Rams, were ready to make a deal for him, but it loomed unlikely a loser would risk the disfavor of its press and fans by trading away such a great gate attraction.

Meanwhile, Simpson was starring for a team, USC, which was in the running for all honors on its level. The Trojans resumed their drive on the first Saturday afternoon in November on a rainy day and a wet, sloppy field at Eugene, Oregon, where 33,500 fans filled the small arena in hopes the Ducks could pull off an upset. They almost did. They tackled O.J. on every Trojan offensive play, whether or not he had the ball, and they held him, and the field held him, to 67 yards in twenty-five carries, lowest of his career. With this, the Ducks had the Trojans on the ropes.

Steve Sogge's passes had kept SC alive, but Oregon had the Trojans tied at 13–13 with less than five minutes left. Oregon's Eric Olsen then hit Greg Lindsay with a pass that went 61 yards to the Southern Cal 38, but when Battle belted him hard, the Duck fumbled and the Trojans took over. Sogge than started to throw. Gambling on fourth down and 2 yards to go from his 46, he hit Klein for 16 yards and the first down to keep things going. Sogge then bombed Lawrence near the goal line, but the ball was batted down. However, an interference call on Oregon's Jim Franklin gave the Trojans a first down on the 3. Sogge targeted Klein in the end zone with 1:12 to play and SC escaped, 20–13.

Oregon's coach Jim Frei said, "I thought if we could stop Simpson, we could stop them. Well, it almost worked." A shaken Southern Cal coach McKay said, "Maybe we didn't give the ball to Simpson enough." Simpson said, "I guess you gotta' play like that once in a while." He shook his head and smiled wistfully. "We were very lucky," he said. "But we did win. And we proved we can win without me doing well. It wasn't me, it was the other guys that won this one, that's for sure."

A week later, at home in 82-degree weather before 80,000 fans, Simpson sizzled, carrying thirty-one times for 164 yards as the Trojans trimmed Cal, 35–17. The Bears had held seven previous foes to only 39 points and they held Simpson to 21 yards in the first half, but he snapped his slump and broke their backs in the second half.

Actually, the Trojans faked to him a lot in the first half. The Bears keyed on him and Sogge passed to others instead. Then McKay dictated a return to Simpson in the second half and an unsure Cal defense was put to rout. Simpson scored twice and Sogge scored three times with passes and when the score reached 35–3 McKay substituted freely.

Later Simpson sat with a bruised thigh, twisted knee, and strained ankle, smiled and said, "You name it and I got it. They hit hard. Maybe it wasn't a hard game, but it sure felt hard out there. It's never easy, you know. And the next one may be the hardest one yet."

Oregon State, 3–0 upset victor over Southern Cal the season before, had handed UCLA its fifth loss in six games, 45–21, this day, and now it was the Beavers who blocked the Trojans' path to the Rose Bowl. The winner would go to Pasadena.

Now, in mid-November, rotund Dee Andros and his rugged Beavers, led by bruising fullback Bill Enyart, came to the Coliseum and battled the Trojans to a standstill as nearly 60,000 L.A. fans fell limp with frustration.

Asked his strategy going in, McKay cracked, "Maybe I'll give the ball to O.J., every play." In the

CONCLUDING A CAREER

first part of the game, he did almost that. O.J. got the ball again and again. And he tore off tremendous yardage. But he could not break free. And SC could not score. Nor could the visitors missing three field goals. At halftime, the tense tussle was scoreless.

In the third quarter, Oregon State took it in, Enyart bucking over for a 7–0 lead.

In the final quarter, the Trojans took over on their own 36. Sogge sneaked 18 yards. Simpson snapped off a 22-yarder. Sogge threw to Terry DeKraii 22 yards for a touchdown and Ayala kicked the tying point, 7–7.

Then SC drove 66 yards, mostly on Simpson runs, to a 21-yard field goal by Ayala that made it 10–7.

Then Sandy Durko intercepted a Steve Preece pass to bring the ball back to SC. And Simpson took off on a fast, flashy 40-yard run that put the Trojans out of reach, 17–7.

He went wide right, DeKraii blocked in the tackle, Scott blocked out the linebacker and O.J. went in between.

A late 74-yard scoring-pass play, Preece to Billy Main, left Oregon State still shy, 17–13. The Beavers tried an onside kickoff, but USC recovered it and Simpson ran 25 yards deep into Beaver territory at the finish. He was pulled down by a desperation grab at his jersey or he would have gone all the way. On his forty-seventh and last carry he carried two huge foes on his back 10 yards.

The home fans stood and screamed for him as he trotted tired off the field. For the second time this season he had carried the ball an awesome forty-seven times and he had run up his one-game high of 238 yards. He had scored his eighteenth touchdown of the season—a spectacular one of 40 yards that had settled the issue near the finish.

The Trojans ran off in triumph, celebrating the clinching of a Rose Bowl berth.

In the dressing room, a reporter asked Simpson, "Why do you always win in the last quarter?"

O.J. smiled and said, "We kind of like it better than losing in the last quarter."

Laughing, he added, "We've met the challenge all year. We fool around and fall behind, but we always come back. That's the mark of a great team.

"You carried the ball forty-seven times," it was pointed out. "Isn't that a lot?"

"It's not a little," Simpson smiled.

"Aren't you tired?"

"I'll just sit here until next week and I'll be fine," O.J. said.

"You set a personal record for ground gained in one game."

"If they'd give it to me ten more times, I'd gain a few more yards, too," Simpson said, "Of course, I'd be dead, but the yards would be good."

McKay was asked how Simpson did it.

John said, "If I knew what he was doing, I'd teach it to someone else next year. As long as I've got him, I'm gonna keep giving him the ball and let him keep doing it, however."

Tom Hamilton, the commissioner of the Pac-8, came in to congratulate the coach, commenting, "You are going to Pasadena to represent us again."

McKay said, "Thanks, Tom. We kind of look on it as a second home."

The Rose Bowl berth had been resolved in their favor, but the national title and an undefeated season remained at stake with two games to play—UCLA and Notre Dame. Undefeated Ohio State, the likely foe in the bowl, and undefeated Penn State remained in the running for the number-one ranking.

Disappointing UCLA had lost four straight games and six out of nine entering the traditional intracity contest, but Tommy Prothro's team was pitched high to salvage a lot from the season by knocking the Trojans from the ranks of the unbeatens.

And they scored first on an Andrusyshyn field goal, 32 yards, for a 3–0 lead. It was the second quarter before USC untracked. Simpson was being run again and again once more and he spearheaded a drive that ended with his 4-yard run and a 7–3 lead. However, Mickey Cureton carried the kickoff back 68 yards and wound up diving over from the 1 to put UCLA back on top 10–7. Another drive pushed by Simpson and another 4-yard run and the Trojans went to intermission ahead, 14–10.

More than 75,000 fans, surprised by the closeness of the contest, saw SC go ahead, 21–10, in the third quarter as the Trojans moved in close, then scored as Sogge faked to Simpson and pitched out to Scott. As Simpson was tackled, Scott ran into the end zone, and Simpson arose to applaud. UCLA closed back in during the last period as Cureton ran 57 yards to set up a score, then 9 to net it, but a 2-point conversion try failed and the Bruins remained behind, 21–16.

Southern Cal settled it with one of its Simpson marches. On his last three carries, he ran for 47 yards. On the last four plays of the march, it was Jay, as he sometimes was called, for 17, Scott for 10, Jay for 26, and then Jay around end for 4 and a 28–16 final score. The Trojan white horse hurried triumphantly around the track, the school song was played, and USC alums and students sang and cheered.

Simpson had carried forty times for 205 yards. He also caught three passes. He scored three touchdowns, giving him twenty-five for the season, surpassing the school record of 24 set by Mort Kaer in 1925. And he reached 234 carries and 1,654 to set new NCAA one-season standards with two games still to go. He had averaged thirty-four carries and 183 yards each game, an incredible pace.

Strangely, now just as they were about to take all the laurels they so much wanted, there was a switch in strategy which hurt the Trojans heavily. Possibly feeling the other teams were keying on Simpson, SC stopped giving him the ball as much as it had been. Up until then, keyed on or not, Simpson got the ball thirty to forty or more times a game, he gained 160 to 200 or more yards a game, and the Trojans won. Three times he had been given the ball forty or more times and each time the Trojans won a big game. The only time he had been given the ball less than thirty times, the Trojans almost lost. Now the ball was given to him less than thirty times two games in a row and the Trojans won neither.

Simpson went into the Notre Dame game with the Heisman Trophy. He was announced the winner by a runaway margin, 855 first-place votes to 49 for runner-up Keyes in balloting by sportswriters and broadcasters across the country. "It is a great thrill," he said. "I've been waiting for it for a year," he grinned.

CONCLUDING A CAREER

But he was given the ball only twenty-one times against the Fighting Irish in the Coliseum and gained only 55 yards, the low of his entire college career. At twenty or twenty-one carries he usually is only warming up. It is in the next ten carries that he usually begins to break away for most of his yardage. And sometimes in additional carries that he pours it on. John McKay had admitted, "If I don't have O.J. carrying thirty-five to forty times a game, it would be like having Joe DiMaggio on your team and only letting him go to bat once a game." Well, O.J. barely got to bat against Notre Dame and the Trojans were tied 21–21 before 82,659 stunned fans. USC fell below undefeated Ohio State and Penn State in the national ratings.

In the first minute, Mickey Durko returned an interception 21 yards to put USC on top, 7–0. But quarterback Joe Theisman led the Irish on two touchdown drives and Bob Gladieux broke off a 57-yard scoring run and at intermission Notre Dame led, 21–7.

In the second half, Southern Cal stormed back. A march finished off by a short run by Simpson cut the margin to 21–14 in the third quarter. A long pass play, 60 yards, Sogge to Dickerson, tied it, 21–21.

Two Notre Dame field-goal attempts in the final half failed and the gun cracked with the clubs square.

After the game, Simpson's No. 32 jersey was ceremoniously retired at midfield. Simpson said, "I'd like to borrow it back for just one more game—the Rose Bowl game against Ohio State."

He sat in deep disappointment in the dressing room later and said, "It was a tough game. They're a tough team. They stopped me. Only I wish I'd run more."

McKay shrugged sadly and said, "It was circumstances. We fell far behind and had to play catch-up by passing a lot."

Notre Dame coach Ara Parseghian said, "We keyed on him and stopped him and we're relieved they didn't run him more. But still, we didn't win. We had them and we lost them."

Mike McCoy, Notre Dame's giant All-American tackle, said, "We held him down, but if they'd run him more, it would have gotten harder and harder. Keyes is all-around, Simpson is class. O.J. deserves the Heisman. Even stopped, he seemed super."

The handful of yards he had gained, by Simpson's standards, nevertheless were enough to make him the all-time Trojan rushing leader. In two years and with one game to go he had gained 3,252 yards, while Mike Garrett in three full years had gained 3,221.

O.J. also had clinched his second straight NCAA rushing championship with 1709 yards.

He already had set a new single-season rushing record in NCAA play and needed only 42 yards to establish a new career mark.

Although he carried the ball only twenty-eight times against Ohio State in the Rose Bowl, he ran for 171 yards to raise his single-season record to 1,880 yards and set the career record at 3,423 yards.

It was one of his greatest and at the same time saddest days for this young man, newly a father, of a daughter.

A crowd of 102,063 persons, including recently elected President Richard Nixon and his family, filled the

Rose Bowl on January 1, 1969, for the fifty-fifth renewal of the oldest of the New Year's Day college classics.

Following the gala parade, the bands marched, the banners flew, and the crowd cheered as the two teams took the field in southern California's winter sunshine.

Undefeated Ohio State was out to protect its number-one ranking and mythical national title. Undefeated but once-tied USC was out to regain the top spot and the college crown.

At the outset, the Trojans stormed the Buckeyes. An 80-yard touchdown run by Simpson and a field goal by Ayala put the Trojans on top, 10–0.

Simpson's scoring run was sensational. He shot through a hole on the left side of his line, angled left through tacklers, then, confronted by defenders, made a sharp cut to the right that threw his foes off-stride, ran against the grain through players who could not alter their direction as artfully as he, through arms, burst into the open, and sped to the goal line as the hometown rooters stood and screamed.

Later, the incomparable coach Bud Wilkinson commented, "I still can't believe Simpson's run. I can't even believe his cut. He made a ninety-degree cut without losing a step. If you saw this type of play in a movie, you would laugh. I still don't believe it. It was utterly unbelievable. I didn't see every back who ever played college ball, but he's the best I've ever seen."

Perhaps the Trojans had gone too far ahead too soon. They seemed to relax. Stung, a strong Ohio State team, whipped into a frenzy by Woody Hayes, their tough coach, stormed back.

Rex Kern, the quarterback, led a devastating attack. He threw two touchdown passes and directed other scoring drives. Jack Tatum sparked a defense which cut off the Trojan offense. Fumbles by Sogge and Simpson led to decisive Ohio State touchdowns. The Buckeyes caught up and poured it on in the second half.

Ohio State won, 27–10. The Bucks were crowned national titleholders. Penn State, which squeezed past Kansas, 15–14, in the Orange Bowl to remain undefeated, too, took the number-two slot. Southern Cal, concluding at 9–1–1, ranked third.

In two seasons with Simpson, Southern Cal had won nineteen games, lost two and tied one. This season, they outscored their foes 255–168. In two seasons, they had outscored them 513–255.

McKay shook Simpson's hand. Then he said, "This is a man I will miss. He has to be the greatest player I ever had, probably the best anyone ever had. He did everything I asked of him. He did more than I asked of him. He was never a bit of trouble to me. He has character. He has been a great player and he is a fine young man."

The Trojan quarters were hushed, the players sitting about in deep disappointment. Simpson spoke softly. He said, "Coming off the field, it's difficult to explain how I felt. This has been the biggest two years of my life. More than anything else, I wanted to come off a winner. It felt terrible to come off a loser. But it has been a good season and a great two seasons and I suppose I shouldn't complain."

In the excited tumult that was the Ohio State dressing room, Woody Hayes said, "O.J. Simpson is a great player and USC is a great team. They had us down, but we came back. We have great players and a great team, too." Buckeye Jack Tatum said, "O.J.'s run was the quickest I ever saw. His cut was too much. He made us play harder. He almost beats you by himself."

Had he carried more, USC might have controlled the ball more and held on better. As it was, his 171 yards in twenty-eight carries gave him an average of more than 6 yards a carry, the second-highest of his twenty-one-game college career. He also caught eight passes for 85 yards in the game to give him 256 yards in total offense in the contest and 2,091 yards in total offense on the season. He had rushed 383 times for 1,880 yards, both new one-season NCAA records.

Suddenly, it was all over. He sat in front of the locker in the dressing room in Pasadena as if he did not want it to end, as if by waiting awhile he could forestall what already had happened—the coming to an end of his short, spectacular college career. Finally, he got up, stripped off his Cardinal and Gold for the last time, and went to shower.

He emerged to put on his civvies. He walked out of the dressing room into the night and into the arms of family and friends and fans and stood for a long time signing autographs and smiling as best he could. It had ended, what was soon to be called the greatest college career of any football player in the 1960's, and what some consider the classic college career of all time.

9 The Greatest Collegian

You do not measure an athlete by statistics alone, but the numbers are enormously impressive in the case of O.J. Simpson's college football career at the University of Southern California. He accomplished more in two seasons, even missing one game one season, than any other runner had managed in three.

In his first season, Simpson rushed 291 times for 1,543 yards, averaging twenty-nine carries and 150 yards per game. In his second season, Simpson rushed 383 times for 1,880 yards, averaging thirty-four carries and 170 yards an outing. He led the nation in rushing both seasons. He set NCAA records for rushes and yards gained the second season.

His career totals of 674 carries for 3,423 yards also set new NCAA records. He averaged thirty-two carries and 163 yards a game for the twenty-one games of his entire career. He carried the ball less than twenty times only in the first game of his career. He carried it thirty or more times fourteen times, forty or more times three times. Twice he carried forty-seven times in games.

O.J. gained less than 100 yards only four times in twenty-one games. He gained less than 150 yards in only one other game. He gained 150 or more yards in sixteen games, 170 or more yards in eleven games, 200 or more yards in five games, with highs of 238, 236, and 235 yards in individual games. He averages less than 5 yards a rush in only six of his twenty-one games Three games he averaged more than 6 yards a rush.

He caught twenty-six passes for 320 yards his senior season, and thirty-six passes for 439 yards in his two seasons. He went over 2,000 yards in total offense his second season and over 3,600 yards in total offense his two seasons. He also set school records with twenty-three touchdowns and 138 points in one season and thirty-six touchdown runs and 216 points in his career.

If you wish to include his two seasons in junior college competition, his four years of college play produced nearly 6,000 yards rushing and ninety touchdowns.

Simpson made every All-American team for the second straight season, of course. He won almost every honor he had missed, including the Heisman Trophy, and was selected Player of the Year by all the major wire service polls and private club committees.

As the 1960's came to a close later, additional laurels were heaped on him. He was voted to the all-time Rose Bowl team, finishing second in the balloting to Don Hutson, the immortal end from Alabama's teams of the 1930's.

O.J. was voted Player of the Decade in a poll in which he surpassed such other stars of the 1960's as Texas' Tommy Nobis, Purdue's Leroy Keyes and Navy's Roger Staubach.

Finally, Simpson joined such men as Sammy Baugh, Red Grange, Jim Thorpe and Bronco Nagurski on an

All-Time All America team selected in a poll by *The Football News*. Simpson, Nobis, Jim Parker, and Chuck Bednarik were the only players from the 1960's selected. Most of the players picked came from the 1920's. The next-most from the 1930's. It was a select group.

Finishing his finest season, O.J. Simpson sat in his apartment, sighed, and confessed, "This has been my hardest year. It was my toughest season. The pressure just kept getting heavier and heavier. I tried not to let on, but it got to me. The press never let me alone for a minute. I always was decent to them and they have been decent to me, but they just kept coming and I never had a moment to myself. The fans and other people kept crowding around. Sometimes it seemed like I couldn't draw a deep breath.

"I carried the ball more than any man before me. Just running it was tiring. The opposition was pointing for me and keying on me and hitting me on almost every play, even when I wasn't carrying the ball. When I was, they would hit me as hard as they could. Naturally, they wanted to slow me down. I hit them hard trying to slow them down. This hurt me, too.

"Players would hit me when I was going down and pile on when I was down. They'd whack me and pull me and twist me. I never said anything to them or anyone else about it. Most played me fair. Many tried to get me out of the game. This is a brutal sport. Anytime you've got two-hundred-and-fifty-pounders hitting people hard it has to be seen it's brutal.

"We had a good team and the tension of sustaining our winning streaks, our undefeated status, our na-

THE GREATEST COLLEGIAN

tional ranking was tremendous. Every game was crucial, every one a war, and it wore us out mentally as well as physically. Physically, I suffered a lot of little injuries—my thigh, my knee, my calf, my ankle. I had to play hurt. And I was bruised and sore and tired after every game.

"Sometimes I'd run better tired. Fresh early in a game, I'd try to be too cute, too fancy. I'd try to think my runs. The bumps would hurt too much. But by the second half I'd be used to the bumps and wouldn't feel them too much. I'd be tired and I'd just run, natural like. Nothing fancy. Just what came natural. And I'd do better.

"The bumps and bruises would begin to hurt that night. My legs would get sore. We'd go out, my wife and I, to a movie or a party, to unwind, to let down a little, and I'd try to stretch the evening out because I didn't want to go home. I'd get home, I'd sit up half the night watching TV because I didn't want to go to bed. I'd go to bed, I couldn't get to sleep. Mental tension. And physical pain. Every place I'd lay, every way I'd turn, I'd feel pain. I spent a lot of sleepless nights, suffering. The next day would be awful. It would take half the week to get back to normal."

He shook his shoulders a little and leaned forward. He said, "I'm not complaining. This is just the way it was. I enjoyed it, but there was a lot of suffering that went with the enjoyment. It was a tremendous satisfaction. I did well and I accomplished a lot and I helped my team accomplish big things. In some ways it was more fun in JC. I was an outside runner. Here, it was inside, inside, inside. But it was a satisfaction grinding out those yards against the best defenses in college ball and a thrill when I broke away for long ones.

"How does it feel to make a long, scoring run through a broken field with the crowd cheering you? It feels fantastic. Kids dream of it, of course. To do it is something else. You don't think of it when you're doing it. You're too occupied. It's bang, bang, bang. You see things happening and you react. When it's over, it's a relief. You look around to see if the ref threw a flag wiping it out. If not, you're ten feet tall. You hear the cheers then. You think, man, I showed them something. It brings out the pride in you. When you see the films you're surprised at some of the moves you made. It has to be instinctive.

"I never even knew I could run inside until I got to USC. They made me into an inside runner. Now I know I can run inside as well as outside. Not all backs can. I can do most of the things most good backs do. I can't do what Jim Brown did because he was two hundred and twenty-eight pounds and I'm not, I get down to below two hundred pounds by the time the season ends. I can't run over people the way he could. But I'm strong enough to run through people, through the arms of tacklers if they don't put on a good tackle, if they don't get a good grip on me. I let my legs go loose and they slide off.

"The running back I've admired the most is Gale Sayers. Another great one has been Leroy Kelly. Sayers is fast and Kelly is quick. Sayers has a million moves, while Kelly makes the sharpest cuts. Hugh McElhenny ran real smart. He followed blockers beautifully. In an open field, he'd glide and pick his spots. Dick Bass was like a little rubber ball—he bounced. I took little things from all of these, but I didn't really copy any of them. I'm built different than them and I have different assets. I came into my own style naturally.

"I hit a hole quick and hard. I try not to hesitate. I try to make my moves right now, decisively. When I get in the open I know I have the speed to run away from anyone. I usually have good condition. My legs are slender, but strong. I have a big upper body. I seem to be able to keep going a speed when others slow down. I don't know why. I'm very determined. A lot of this game is mental. I think my reputation psyched a lot of guys out. They went in thinking they couldn't stop me, so they couldn't. But I came up to the challenges. I usually had my best games against the best teams. When I wasn't inspired I let down a little.

"I want to be an artist at my trade. I study backs and try to be smart. I'm always imagining situations, dreaming them up in my mind, and figuring out how to escape them. I'm always carrying a game around with me. I take a game home and brood over it. I'm very self-critical. I'm never satisfied. I'm always thinking of what I did right and what I did wrong. The writers come up to me and praise me after almost every game, but I know the games I rated praise and the ones I didn't. On Sunday mornings I'd pick up a paper and read how great I'd been when inside I'd know all the mistakes I made."

He leaned back and looked up as though his eyes were on a distant star. He spoke of pro ball. He said, "I don't ever want to go through a year like this past year.

But next year could be harder to get through. The pros are the best. I'm apt to wind up with one of the worst. It's going to be tough. Pro defenders are bigger and faster and smarter than most college defenders. I know I'll be singled out. But I've been singled out for two years now and I survived.

"I'm sure they'll test me. I'll just have to get up and come back for more. I'll just have to earn their respect. I think it may not be physically as rough in pro ball. I'm sure I'll carry the ball less. And I think if pros respect you, they'll hit you hard but fair. That's the impression I get. I think they're the best football players in the world and they're all playing for a living and they have a feeling for one another.

"Any back who carries the ball a lot is bound to get hurt sooner or later. You just hope it won't be too often and it won't be too bad. I saw Sayers wreck his knee on TV film. Some said it didn't look that bad, but I knew right away it was bad because he had his feet planted when he was hit from the side. A back can be hurt other ways, but it's freakish then. Usually, you get hurt when your feet are planted. I almost got hurt like that against Stanford. But my cleats tore loose and I was able to roll with the blow. That's all you can do, try to roll with the blow.

"Against Indiana in the Rose Bowl, I was carrying a guy on my back when I got hit from the front. I was dug in so deep, I could have torn up my leg. But my cleats gave way as I went down. I went down thinking I must have been hurt. I felt my leg. I stood up and tested it. I couldn't believe I was OK. The only time I was hurt in college ball was in my junior year when someone stepped on my foot and it tore up my instep, which was freakish. I've been fortunate so far. I'm willing to wait awhile for my luck to turn," he smiled.

"I can get up for most games. I know when I'm up. I'm not uptight like some cats. Not sick or anything like that. I'm loose. McCullouch and I used to joke with one another. Some of the other cats would look at us like we were crazy. But that way we were ready. I'd get a little nervous, anxious to prove myself, but confident. The first hit would relax me and I'd be going.

"I've watched the pros play and I think I can play with them. Some say I'll star. We'll have to see about that. We'll have to see what team I go with. It's hard to star with a bad team. I'm not used to losing. I don't know how I'd handle that. I wouldn't want to get discouraged. I wouldn't want to get down. I know with my reputation a lot will be expected of me. But I'll need help to give what I got to give. I know anything less than an exceptional year will disappoint a lot of people. That puts a lot of pressure on me.

"I don't feel I owe football anything. You get out of it what you put into it. I've given it a lot and now it's going to give me back. I want a good contract. This is my one chance to bargain. I worked hard to get on top and I want it to pay off. I come from the lower class. I never had much. I want to have everything else anyone else has. My real motivation is not money. It's to be known as the best. Success and recognition inspires me. But I'm moving up to the pay window now and I want those checks to be fat. I've got to protect my family and my future and this may be the one real chance I'll have in my lifetime."

10 Reaching for a Rainbow

Losing twelve games, tying one, and winning only one, Buffalo won the big one—the right to draft first and take O.J. Simpson out of college ranks. A headline read: BILLS COME THROUGH. LOSE GAME AND WIN SIMPSON. Philadelphia finished second in the race to be last in pro football and first in line. The Eagles lost twelve, but won two. Another headline read: EAGLES BLOW THE BIG ONE. WIN THE GAME. A writer wrote, "The Eagles can't win except when they want to lose. They are so inept they can't even lose right." Atlanta also lost twelve and won two. Pittsburgh finished fourth in this special race, losing eleven, tying one, and winning two. But Atlanta and Pittsburgh were teams with potential. Had they lost just one more and landed Simpson, a few years later he would have been running for a contender.

Buffalo was an old city with an old stadium. After it selected Simpson, a *Sports Illustrated* spread presented it as a soiled city with an ancient arena. When it received a new coat of paint a few years earlier, Jimmy Cannon wrote, "That is like putting rouge on a corpse." It was in a bad part of town and customers were afraid to park outside. Not only was there looting and vandalism, but a Bills' vice-president was knifed after one game. The locker rooms leaked so badly

Detroit coach Joe Schmidt once had his players dress in their hotel.

Dispiritedly, Simpson recoiled from this situation. He said, "I'm a Californian. I love this beautiful state. I love warm weather. I'm not looking forward to going all the way east to Buffalo. I hear it gets very cold and snows there. But what can I do? The draft is not very democratic. The system isn't fair. The player has no freedom of choice where he'll live or which team he'll play for. But that's the system and I have to live in it. I'll have to make the best of it. It's a weak team, but it's bringing in a new coach, John Rauch, who was a winner in Oakland. Maybe I can help it become a winner.

"If I make big money it will help. I may be the first of my race to really cash in. I don't plan to play forever. I'd like to play for about five years, then quit to work with kids, ghetto kids who need help. Ghetto kids respect money. They respect the guy with the bankroll, the fancy clothes, and the big car. If that man tells them something, they'll listen. They figure he beat the system. They figure he knows how to make it. Which is why a lot of bad men—criminals and pushers and pimps—are heroes in some ghettos. It's the making it that matters. They look at the average playground leader and see how he's scratching to survive so they figure what does he know? Well I want to make it in a clean thing, sports, and go back and show the kids I made it and work with them so they'll get their chance."

O.J. needed a manager. Every athletes' agent, athletes' lawyer, athletes' manager around was after him and he needed one, but he didn't know which one. He not only had to negotiate a contract with Buffalo, but he was flooded with offers to endorse products, represent firms, make appearances, cut commercials, and so forth and he had no way of knowing which ones to accept and which to reject. He had met Chuck Barnes, a USC graduate, at the school. He had been impressed with him. Barnes operated Sports Headliners, Inc., and had made money for race drivers A.J. Foyt, Parnelli Jones, and Mario Andretti. He had negotiated Earl McCullouch's contract with Detroit. John Unitas had joined him. Simpson signed with Barnes.

In sixty days, he received 340 requests for Simpson's services. In sixty days, O.J. filled forty-five of them.

Barnes was only thirty-eight. He was trim and looked athletic. He smoked a pipe and seemed studious. He was soft-spoken and friendly. He lulled you with his casual air. But he was very shrewd and sharp and could get tough if necessary to close a difficult deal.

His father retired as president of Dayton Tire & Rubber Company, a Firestone subsidiary. Chuck was born in Kalamazoo, Michigan, but moved around a lot as a boy as his father shifted here and there. Chuck attended a prep school in Louisiana and graduated from a high school in Ohio.

He graduated from USC and went to work for Firestone, following in his father's footsteps. However, he went out on his own after meeting driving champion Rodger Ward, who wanted a personal manager. Barnes added Foyt and Jones and formed his firm in Indianapolis in January of 1964. Andretti and others joined up.

Barnes says, "As a general rule, race drivers, the top ones, can make more money than other athletes. They can win big purses, but that's only part of it. Auto racing lends itself to sponsorships more than other sports. Endorsing everything from tires to crash helmets, from spark plugs to fuel, a top driver can make a quarter of a million dollars before he ever turns a wheel.

"All top athletes need representation. The owners and commercial firms have the finest legal and business brains at their disposal and it is unreasonable for them to expect unsophisticated athletes, especially youngsters right out of college, to negotiate without experienced help.

"We take our cut from our clients' earnings. This is business. But we limit our clients to only those who need help and we work hard for them. We screen their offers and negotiate their contracts. We get as much for them as we can. No one can force anyone to pay anything that's unreasonable.

"We try to limit each client to a few good things instead of getting him involved in a lot of ordinary things. We want to put him in a position to make as much side money as possible, while freeing him to pursue his sport."

A married man with two daughters, Barnes said, "Simpson is a young man with a young family. His future is at stake. He is worth as much money as any football player who ever entered professional ranks. He is getting a lot of outside offers but we want just a few big things instead of a lot of little things. Right now he needs ready cash for investments. We want to provide tax shelters for him and protection for his future."

Barnes investigated the possibility of O.J. representing Florida Orange Juice, but singer Anita Bryant had a long-term contract to do commercials for and represent that group. Instead he set a three-year deal with Chevrolet for $250,000. This gave Simpson some advance money while waiting for his Bills' salary to be worked out. He also got a Corvette to drive and his wife got a Chevelle. His mother got a Caprice.

Barnes set another deal with ABC-TV for Simpson to serve as a commentator and to do some acting. He did a *Medical Center* show and surprised some critics with his work. A big book deal covering his rookie pro year was negotiated. A fat pact to represent Royal Crown Cola was set: "O.J. for R.C."

Meanwhile, Barnes met with Ralph Wilson, owner of the Buffalo Bills, and made his pitch. He asked for $600,000 for five seasons on a no-cut contract and a $500,000 loan at 5 percent interest for investment purposes. The investments would be in stocks, which would serve as security.

Wilson withdrew as though in shock. Shortly, pro basketball players would demand and receive much fatter contracts. Lew Alcindor, Spencer Haywood, and others were on the verge of signing for more than a million dollars for five or six years. But there was a war on in basketball, where the NBA and ABA were bidding for players, and salaries and bonuses were soaring. There was no war in football, where the NFL and AFL had merged, and players took what was offered or didn't play.

Wilson countered with a flat offer of $350,000 for

four years without any loan. Barnes walked away. As the weeks passed, Wilson went to the press to plead his case to the public. Among others, he sought out Melvin Durslag, the L.A. *Herald-Examiner* columnist. Barnes and Simpson had been sworn to secrecy, but now Wilson revealed details. This served to drive the bargaining parties apart.

Wilson, who owned a trucking concern, a television station, a washing machine company, an insurance firm, and a stable of race horses, in addition to his football team, said, "Their demand was outrageous. I can't get a loan at five percent. And certainly not with the loan serving as collateral. So why should I make such a loan myself? When they come out of orbit and return to earth, I'll talk to them."

Barnes said, "We held our silence until Wilson broke his. We didn't reveal the details, he did. They were substantially correct. And I think our request was fair. Actually, we figured out what O.J. was worth and cut it in half, which certainly is fair. They've never drawn in exhibition games before. Now they're booking the best teams in the biggest arenas. They formerly played preseason games in Tampa, Allentown, and Winston-Salem. After drafting O.J., they signed for exhibitions this season in the L.A. Coliseum, in the Houston Astrodome, and as part of a doubleheader in Cleveland Stadium. In L.A., without O.J., they might draw twenty-five thousand fans. With him, they may draw seventy-five thousand. With O.J., exhibition earnings may rise three hundred and fifty thousand dollars. They can make back their money on O.J. in the preseason alone.

"Once the season starts, he will boost them tremendously both at the gate and on the field. They need him. If they don't feel he is worth what we're asking, they can trade him to a team which does. A number of top teams are prepared to meet our figures. If he wants to sell his team, we're prepared to buy it. We'll pay O.J. what he's worth."

Said Wilson, "I am gratified that they are allowing me to keep my other businesses. Let me review: I was one of the original owners in the American League. I accepted the Buffalo franchise without having set foot in the town. In nothing flat, I blew a million, four hundred thousand. I fought the National League. I served on the merger committee that finally brought peace. After all the sweat and headaches our franchise is just beginning to see daylight. And now I would be asked to sell out because I won't give one football player six hundred thousand plus a half-million-dollar loan.

"Simpson will be offered far more than any new player has received since the merger. If he proves he can play with the big boys, his pay will go up even higher. But I have to keep my senses in this thing. I can't let agents walk in and commandeer my team. Nor will I trade him. Teams have expressed an interest in him, but we have an interest in him, too."

Offers for Simpson's services came in from Canadian Football League teams and Continental Football League teams. The latter was a minor league, but the owners of the team in Indianapolis, Barnes' "hometown," were prepared to pay Simpson a bonus of $100,000, a base salary of $150,000, and a loan of $500,000 for one season's play, feeling swollen gate receipts around the circuit would more than make up for it and enhance the possibility of some of the cities crashing the big-time. All would chip in. Ft. Worth and Hawaii also wanted him. Montreal, which had drafted him after his junior college career, was the Canadian club interested in him.

Most laughed at the Continental League offer. Surely, Simpson would not consider beginning in the bushes. Simpson himself laughed. But Barnes insisted he consider it seriously. "If you are a professional and are playing for pay you have to consider the pay and they may be willing to pay you more for one season than anyone else is," he said. "If we are stalemated with Buffalo, this would give us a chance to play one year elsewhere and possibly strengthen our position."

Barnes' business was growing. He was opening offices in New York and Los Angeles and moving into the L.A. office. He was kept busy weighing offers for Simpson. He said, "This is a very special young man. He charms you. He can talk. He has a persuasive personality. Blacks never have had a fair share of advertising or acting roles, but O.J. rises above that and appeals to all."

Wilson said, "Our player budget at Buffalo is roughly a million a year. I would like to give O.J. the million and let him pay all the players, including himself, what they are worth. That way, I would be off the hook. It would be O.J.'s problem to deal with those who get him the ball and block for him."

Simpson said, "I am well aware I need help to help my new team. But I am also aware I will never be in a better bargaining position. I know what I accomplished in college ball and I know my potential for pro ball and I know I am entitled to the kind of terms other highly regarded rookies have gotten in the past.

"I have met Mr. Wilson only once. That was before the draft, but when it was clear Buffalo was going to draft me. I liked him. I thought a pro owner might come on strong, but he didn't. The only thing I didn't like about him was when he made the negotiations public. Having all my personal business spread all over the newspapers embarrasses me.

"A lot of people say I'm asking too much. But a lot of people say I should get all I can. It's not easy to know what to ask for. I know Chuck Barnes investigated what other rookies received and I know he asked for less. I trust him to negotiate for me."

He sighed and said, "I just wish it would be wound up. I'm tired of all the talk."

But it went on and on and on for weeks and weeks and months and months, a hot sports topic, unresolved.

Meanwhile, O.J.'s pro potential was debated. Simpson's hero, Gale Sayers, surprised the youngster by speaking against his chances: "He's a fine back," said Sayers, "but he doesn't impress me as having outside speed. He sees holes and hits them and gets out fast. But O.J. will find it's a completely different game with the pros. He's fumbled a lot, so I don't know if he has the good hands of a receiver. And he'll have a lot to learn. He'll have to learn to block. He'll have to learn to read more complicated defenses than he faced in college ball."

At a Philadelphia banquet, after listening to Sayers put him down, Simpson got up, smiled, and said, "He's right. I have a lot to learn. And Sayers is a master. A genius at solving defenses." Then, with a mischievous smile he added, "But I don't think I'm dumber than any others. . . ." And everyone laughed. George Allen, the Los Angeles coach at the time, and a reserved man normally where rookies were concerned, said, "I don't think anyone has to concern themselves about Simpson as a pro. He is bigger than Sayers and faster than Kelly. He is smart and tough. He is tremendous."

Sid Gillman, coach of the San Diego team, said, "O.J. made it the day he was born. He was just born to run."

11 Life-Style of a Star

O.J. Simpson is flying to San Diego. He is kidding a pretty blond stewardess. He asks her if she's been sampling the little bottles of liquor they serve on airplanes. She giggles, "Would that be any way to run an airline?"

The stewardess asks to see his watch, a handsome one he was gifted by the Frairs Club. He shows it to her and smiles and says, "I always get watches. Let's see, I gave one to my uncle, one to my brother-in-law. I'm saving one for my son. Gonna have a son some day."

One by one the people on the plane recognize him. "I thought so," yells a woman. "It's Orange Juice Simpson!" Soon they are going at him, getting autographs, which he gives out with patience and smiles.

He was wearing a turtleneck shirt under a sports coat. In the hotel he changes to a white shirt and blazer, but he can't decide what tie to wear. He dumps a pile out of a suitcase onto a bed. "I just never know what tie to wear so I bring 'em all along," he says.

He heads out for the "Banquet of Champions." A lot of local pro stars are introduced ahead of him—Billy Casper, Elvin Hayes, Lance Alworth, and others. Then it is his turn. "All the way with O.J.," the announcer says. Simpson stands up to applause, "California's Athlete of the Year."

Hands folded in front of him, he gives a commercial pitch for USC and John McKay, who recruits athletes from this area. Then he talks of his career. And his problems signing with Buffalo.

Sid Gillman, coach of the Chargers, is in the audience. "If Sid Gillman can swing a deal to get me here from Buffalo, I'll pay the rent at his stadium," Simpson smiles. Gillman and the others in the audience laugh.

Afterwards a group from La Jolla High corner him. O.J. says, "La Jolla. Dick Allmon, our center, came from that school. And Raquel Welch. Yaaa, yaa, Raquel Welch."

It is time to run. He is late for a plane to Chicago. On the plane from San Diego to L.A., the pilot radios ahead. Yes, for O.J. Simpson the flight to Chicago can be held. In L.A. an airport car speeds him wildly to his plane. "That man was trying to help, but he darn near killed us," O.J. sighs.

The plane arrives in Chicago at 5:50 A.M. Simpson, who seldom sleeps in planes, has slept a little on this one. He gets off and it is cold. Someone says, "Damned cold." Simpson smiles and says, "But not as cold as Buffalo."

From a dinner in Chicago he flies to a dinner in Detroit. It is snowing in Detroit. Driving to the hotel, O.J. laughs and says, "I am going to have it put in my contract with Buffalo that it won't snow during football season." He sort of sings, "Forget the snow . . . in Buffalo."

He is always asking the writers what they think of Buffalo, and is always depressed when they say they don't like it. He is confronted by writers and broadcasters wherever he goes. And he signs a hundred autographs everywhere he stops.

In Detroit, he does a sports show for Chevrolet. "It's not just that they're paying me to represent them," he says diplomatically. "The first car I owned was a fifty-seven Chevy. Then I had a sixty-one Chevy." The broadcaster beams.

Afterwards, at a party, the ad men slap him on the back and shake his hand and say, "Great, O.J. You were marvelous. Wonderful."

"I almost blew it," he whispers to a friend. "In one part I almost said 'Firebird' instead of 'Camaro.' "

At the Press Club stag dinner that night, he gets a bigger hand than the mayor, the governor, the senators, or other celebrities who are present. But he almost has to shake himself awake to give his speech. He no longer is even certain where he is.

Later, he sips ginger ales because they have no R.C. Colas. He says he could endorse ginger ale, too.

Then he boards a plane for San Francisco. He stretches out his long legs. He laughs and says, "A guy in Houston last week asked me if anything had changed in my life. I told him one thing had changed. Definitely. I don't go coach any more. I go first-class now, all the way."

The plane comes in over the Bay. It lands in this city where O.J. Simpson grew up in poverty. He is picked up and the car speeds past Candlestick Park, where Simpson hawked cushions as a kid. He arrives where he is to speak to the Guardsmen, a group of 150 San Francisco civic and business leaders who devote their spare time to helping kids by sending them to summer camps.

O.J. says, "I believe we must walk the middle of the road on the race issues, not be too militant or too conservative. We should let the kids work it out. Kids aren't born with prejudice. They can get along with anybody if someone doesn't interfere. It's pretty tough to find kids who don't like other kids. The color doesn't matter."

He says, "A lot of kids shy away from school. I know I did. I think we should make it fun to learn at these camps. Bring in a mechanic to talk about cars, a doctor to discuss medicine. Let the kids do what they want. The instructors would be not only teachers, but counselors."

He speaks of his own plans for his own camp. He says, "We have to give these kids some reason to stay in school, some goal."

The Guardsmen seem moved by his speech. They respond with warmth.

Simpson is taken to a television station where he has agreed to cut some commercials for the group. It takes several takes to get two right. Simpson smiles and says, "They usually call me 'One-Take Simpson.' This is gonna' ruin my reputation."

Finished, he signs five footballs to be raffled off for $50 apiece.

In his hotel, O.J. kids the bellhop, an aged man old enough to be his grandfather: "You on a team? Which team you on? I'm always interested in athletes. I know all the big athletes," Simpson says.

The old bellhop looks at him as though he were crazy. A writer, Dwight Chapin of the L.A. *Times*, says, "This is O.J. Simpson, the USC football star."

The bellhop says, "Oh. What position does he play?" Simpson breaks up.

He speaks at a USC alumni party. He is glad to see his old coaches and teammates. In his speech, he says, "They said if you go to UCLA, you're a Bruin for four years, but if you go to USC, you're a Trojan for life."

He gets prolonged applause. He sits down and takes his wife's hand. He says, "I have become more aware of my image lately. I have to stand up in front of people and speak. It's not just playing on the field, but what I project in person. With Chuck Barnes, I'm in a lot of commercial things. I have to do right by the people paying me more than I ever dreamed of making."

He and his wife are among the last to leave. Marguerite says, "O.J.'s always last out. I've spent so many hours waiting for him." He goes to get her coat from the checkroom girl. He asks Chapin for a quarter. He has been bumming change from the writer for days. Chapin reaches for a quarter. "No," O.J. says suddenly. He pulls a dollar bill from his wallet and drops it in the tip tray. He says, "You know, it makes me feel good to be able to use money like that. I'm just learning to do it, you know."

In his Los Angeles apartment, he speaks of the house he is building for Marguerite and their daughter Arnella. He says, "Even if I'm going to play in Buffalo, I'm going to live in L.A.—summers, anyway. So we're getting a fancy home here. I want a swimming pool and a big backyard and a big gaming room. I want to show football movies. We like to entertain friends, barbecue, and play cards. My wife wants a sunken living room and a spiral staircase. It's nice to know you can have what you want.

"My wife likes clothes, so she can buy them now. If I see a sweater I like, I can get it without worrying about price. If I go to a restaurant, I order what I want without seeing how much it costs. If the service is good, I can leave a big tip. I enjoy that. I fly first-class. Not because it's first-class, but because it's more comfortable. I don't care that you're served booze in first class. I don't even drink hard stuff.

"I can go to Vegas and blow fifteen-hundred dollars and not come home worrying myself sick because I put myself in a hole. I went to Vegas and rolled fifteen straight passes with the dice. The newspapers made a big thing of it. They said I only bet a buck a roll and made fifteen dollars. I bet more than that and won more. Not much, only a couple of hundred, but more than a buck a roll. One man bet with me and won thirty thousand dollars and gave me some."

He laughed and said, "I got to figure out how much I'd have made if I started with a buck and let it ride all the way. But I crapped out on the sixteenth roll, so maybe I'd have blown it all."

He shrugged his shoulders, grinning. "I got to know when to be careful and when to quit. I love the horse races and spend a lot of time at the tracks, but when I was blowing a hundred dollars a day for no reason I quit going. When I figure out how much I'm gonna' get, I'm gonna' get together with Barnes and go on a budget. Even the Elvis Presleys have a budget, I think.

"You have to remember I never had money before. Even at USC I lived on a hundred and thirty dollars a month. The school got me some gardening work. Not much. My wife worked as a librarian. In her life, she always had money so this not having much was good for her. Having money now is good for me. My kids will be raised different than I was. I hope having money doesn't spoil them. But they'll get to have the things kid should have. They won't see a struggle. And they'll get their chances to be what they want to be."

He looked at his daughter, who was in a playpen in the middle of the room. He said, "To a person who comes from a lower class, money means a lot. But I'm worried people will look at me differently because I'm asking a lot of money and maybe making a lot of money. I always wanted to be liked and respected. I always wanted when I'd pass people to say, 'That's O.J. I like him. Good football player. Nice person.'

"Living changes you. I've been exposed to better things than I ever knew existed before. I've met good people. I want to be a good person. At one point in my life I looked at life as a jungle where you just had to grab what you could get and hold onto that. I guess in a way that's still true. But I see there's a lot of good things in life if you work hard at whatever you have going for yourself.

"A lot of people I know in the area I came from, a lot of guys I grew up with, see it differently. But it's all in the way you adjust yourself. You know what your capabilities are and you just try to develop them the best you can and you just work from there. Some can't be football players or big businessmen. The individual might happen to drive a truck. But he should determine just what he can do and if it's truck driving he should get the best truck-driving job he can and do the best job he can.

"If you have a good wife and she does the best job she can, you can live within the means of whatever income you're making. You know, everyone can't drive a Cadillac. But you have to accept the fact. A lot of people can't afford one, but they get one anyway and they make life rough on themselves. You have to be able to adjust your mind to get what you can out of life.

"The toughest part of my life is adjusting to my popularity and the stuff that goes with it. Not long ago I enjoyed it. Then I began to tire of it. It's something I always asked for, but sometimes I wish I could just be an ordinary person and be left alone to go my own way and live my life in peace. As a kid you dream of being famous, but when fame comes, well, I guess too much of anything is just too much. You like to be left alone when you're eating, for example. But they come up and ask for an autograph just as you're shoving a forkful of food in your mouth.

"Well, it's the price you have to pay and I don't suppose it's really too high. I'm getting a lot out of it. And I like people. I also like to play tennis and go bowling and wish I could do these things without being mobbed. But I'm in business now. It wasn't so long ago I was about to be photographed drinking a glass of orange juice at USC when a coach stopped me, saying he was sure I wouldn't want to commercialize my football name. Now, that's all I'm doing.

"I'm looking forward to playing. I'm tired of business and want to get back to sport. I'm worried that this thing is dragging on. I want to play pro. I want to prove myself as a pro. I'm worried that going with a weak team, I may not do well. I want to do well. Like Jim Brown, I want to get out while I'm on top, before I get banged up. I don't want to limp away.

"I don't think I have the temperament to coach. Maybe I can act. In any event, I want to work with kids. And I don't want to wait too long. I think it's harder to communicate with kids after you pass thirty. And I think someone like myself who got out of the slum has an obligation to help others get out. I have a special feeling for black kids, of course. I'm black. And I know a black kid has a rougher road to go. I'm not militant, but I'm black. I want people to accept me as a person, not as a black, but I feel an obligation to my people. I believe everything can't be changed at once, but I believe if each of us changes some things it can set off a chain reaction.

"When I go home to meet some of my old classmates, they always want to talk about the past. They only think about the past because they have no futures. They're working at small jobs with no chances for advancement. I tell the kids they shouldn't be satisfied with just getting by. I tell them if they're black and from the lower class it's gonna be tougher for them, but they can make it if they work at it. Even if they're not gonna be athletes, they can make it. They have to have an education. They have to take advantage of every opportunity. They have to have hope for the future. I tell them there's a lot bigger things than being a football star. I tell them there's a lot of big things they can shoot for."

12 Shuffle Off to Buffalo

O.J. Simpson and the Buffalo Bills remained apart through the spring and summer until everyone was weary of the impasse and wondering if it would really be resolved after all. A San Francisco 49er executive excited Simpson by telephoning him a trade was set, but it fell through.

In May, assuming Simpson would be signed, *Sport Magazine* assigned this writer to do a story on O.J. for its preseason issue and had the Bills send a uniform for him so he could be photographed in it for a cover picture.

Arriving at this writer's house, the writer's wife and daughters tried it on first and were photographed in it. Simpson actually got it second.

His first question was, What number was on the jersey? He was happy to hear it was 32, his USC number. This writer said, without thinking, that not many top men had worn that number. "No," O.J. grinned, "only Jim Brown and Sandy Koufax."

Actually, when he got to Buffalo, another player held 32. He was a lesser player and a reserve, but not wanting to cause trouble, Simpson said he'd take another number, and he was given 36. Before the season began, however, the other player was cut, and Simpson got his 32 back.

Barnes agreed to have Simpson meet with Wilson man-to-man, but their talk did not settle matters. In fact, O.J. got angry. Barnes remained unruffled. Later, Simpson said, "Before we went into this Chuck knew there'd be difficulties and times we'd be backed up against a wall and times we might get mad at each other, but we agreed we had to stick together. I'm being offered fifty-thousand dollars a year, which is what other rookies are getting. I know Wilson must have a better figure in mind, but he won't come up. I don't want to, but I'll wait out the season if I have to."

O.J. went out to film *Medical Center*, a story about a college football star who contracts pheochromocytoma, a tumor of the adrenal gland, a malady which threatens his chances to sign a $500,000 pro contract. He sat in a special "Guest Star" chair reading his script. A USC teammate leaned over and asked, "Learning your lines, darling?" USC's Craig Fertig and Willie Brown had been recruited to play in the backfield with O.J. in football scenes and Marv Goux was hired as technical adviser.

They went out on the field. In one shot, O.J. ran through the line and he was brought down, but everyone was cautious and it looked phony. Goux growled, "Don't slide off him, run over him. He's getting paid." Simpson smiled and Barnes shuddered. Simpson was advised to get up slowly after each tackle because he was supposed to have this sickness. Goux said, "You don't have to tell him that. He does it naturally, anyway."

Between scenes, O.J. played touch football with the extras. A lot of people interrupted to ask him for autographs. Some small kids came over. "Hey, you O.J.?" one of them asked.

"Naw," O.J. said. He pointed at Willie Brown. "That's O.J."

"The kids knew better. One asked, "You gonna sign with Buffalo?"

"You think I ought to?" O.J. asked.

"How much you want?"

"How much do you think I'm worth?"

"I wouldn't give you ninety cents, Simpson," one kid said, and laughed.

O.J. smiled and asked, "You play football?"

"Sure," the kid said.

"What position?"

"Quarterback," the kid said proudly.

"I figured you were a quarterback the way you talked," O.J. said.

"C'mom, you gonna sign?"

"I don't know yet, I really don't."

"I'll tell you, Simpson," the quarterback said, "if they pay you a million dollars, you sure ain't gonna be warming no bench."

He wanted to play in the annual College All-Star Game in Chicago against the reigning pro champions but he had not signed so he could not risk appearing in the game and it came and went, the first of August, without him. Sadly, he said, "It'd been a dream of mine since I was a youngster."

The pro teams were in camp now, but Buffalo was without its star rookie. Simpson worried, "I'm not in shape. I'm not ready. I'm afraid if I get too late of a start it'll hurt my first season."

In August, Simpson, his manager, Barnes, and his

attorney, Barnes' associate, David Lockton, went to the San Diego law offices of Don Augustine, who was representing Wilson. They threw onto Augustine's desk a lawsuit they were considering filing against NFL commissioner Pete Rozelle, Buffalo owner Wilson, and the other twenty-five owners, asking for a substantial amount of damages because the draft restricted Simpson to dealing with one club, which would not pay him what he wanted, nor trade him to another club, and because he was not permitted to bargain with a team he wanted to play for, for a price he wanted.

Augustine, who had represented the AFL Players' Association, said he had filed similar suits for his own clients and had a lot of them in his desk drawer. He said one took eight weeks to reach the Supreme Court and suggested that even if O.J. won such a suit he could be a forgotten man by that time. He suggested everything Simpson had or might get depended on his maintaining his status as a player.

The impasse was broken in midmonth. Wilson came up in his offer and Barnes went down in his demands. They agreed on a contract calling for O.J. to receive the $250,000 for four seasons at $55,000 the first season, $60,000 the second, $65,000 the third, and $70,000 the fourth, plus a substantial annuity to come to O.J. at age fifty, and a $150,000 loan for four years.

Relieved, Simpson signed. It was a solid contract, not what he and Barnes had wanted, but better than Wilson had originally offered by far. Without another top team to turn to, stuck with the system, the player has little choice. With Barnes, Simpson had held out as long as he could without risking his career.

"Now, all I want is to play," he sighed.

"I hope the people give him a chance. I hope they don't hold this thing against him. If there has to be a villain in this, it was me, not O.J.," Barnes said.

He need not have worried. Late on the night of August 12, Simpson saw Buffalo for the first time. His plane landed there. A crowd of 2,500 persons waited to welcome him and as he stepped off the plane, they chanted, "All the way with O.J. All the way with O.J." He received a handshake from the mayor and a kiss from a beauty queen.

Self-conscious because he was wearing striped slacks and a gold sports shirt instead of a suit and tie, Simpson apologized for his dress, thanked them for their welcome, and promised to do his best for them and his new team. "I've been trying to get here for six months," he laughed.

Smiling, he shook hands and signed autographs. Jack Horrigan, a Bills' vice-president, got him into a car and drove away with him. Simpson sat quietly, seeing everything there was to be seen about his new city. Later he said, "Look, after L.A. and San Francisco, it didn't look too good. But it didn't look too bad, either. I mean, people make a city, anyway. And I didn't know these people yet."

A city of less than half a million, it barely made the top thirty in the U.S. and was one of the smallest with a major league franchise. However, it had 1,300,000 in its metropolitan area and was an enthusiastic sports town.

In the 1940's, the Bills had a franchise in the All America Conference, which rose up to challenge the

NFL, but it was not one of those taken in by the NFL when the AAC folded. Two which were the Cleveland Browns and San Francisco 49ers. With the formation of the American Football League, the Bills were reborn in 1960. In the middle 1960's, under the coaching of Lou Saban, they won four divisional pennants and two league championships in play-offs from San Diego, primarily with a tough defensive team. Their stars were Tom Sestak, Tom Day, Jim Dunaway, Billy Shaw, George Saimes, George Byrd, quarterback Jack Kemp, and running-back Cookie Gilchrist. There were years when they lost only two or three games.

But Saban left, stars faded, and the team slipped to four victories and ten defeats in 1967 and one victory, one tie, and twelve defeats in 1968. By 1969, Johnny Rauch had been brought in from Oakland where he had won everything but the ultimate titles, but had bristled under the tight reins held by Al Davis. And Rauch faced a difficult rebuilding job. Kemp had a sore arm and the best back-up quarterback, Jim Harris, was inexperienced. There was one good receiver, Haven Moses, and a promising one, Marlin Briscoe. Prior to the arrival of O.J., little Max Anderson was the best runner. Wayne Patrick was the fullback. Bill Enyart was another rookie hopeful. There were a few good linemen such as Jim Dunaway, Paul Costa, and Ron McDole, but there were glaring weaknesses in both the offensive and defensive lines and in the defensive secondary.

War Memorial Stadium was an ancient arena seating fewer than 50,000. Attendance in 1968 had averaged less than 36,000. It was one of the few stadiums on the circuit which was not sold out regularly. Its last two crowds the last season had been less than 30,000. There had been a lot of talk about building a new home for the team, and some veiled threats by Wilson that otherwise he might take his team from town, but not much had come of it.

By the time O.J. arrived at the Niagara University training camp, the Bills had played and split two exhibition games and were a few days away from their third preseason effort against the Lions in Detroit. Rauch shook his hand and to Simpson's surprise sent him off to the photographers. O.J. had expected to be pressured into practice right off, but publicity was important to the pros. Seventeen photographers followed him through his first workout. Buffalo scout Elbert Dubenion said, "He looks smaller than I thought." But Simpson's head was too big for his helmet and they had to send a rush order to USC for his old helmet and to St. Louis to have one like it made up. Trainer Eddie Abramoski said, "I hate for him to wear the wrong helmet." General manager Bob Lustig said, "We'll get him any kind of helmet he wants."

Simpson set to work to learn the plays and to win over his teammates. He admitted, "I was afraid they'd resent me. I was afraid they'd resent my money. I was afraid they'd resent me arriving like some Black saviour to bail their poor team out. Some did. But most were all right with me. I guess they wanted anyone they figured they could win with."

Max Anderson, whose spot Simpson figured to take, said, "He's a nice guy. I can't hate him just because he's a great football player. I'll play my share and he'll play his and the team will be better off for it." Veteran Tom Day said, "O.J. is well schooled. Otherwise, he's like any rookie—a little cocky, but a little shy. We'll warm him up. And cool him off. Before the season starts, we have a ritual with rookies. We shave off all their hair. We'll see how O.J. takes that. He's got to film all those commercials, you know."

O.J. took it just fine. On order, he stood up in the dining room and sang the school song, badly, for which he was razzed. He took the razzing and returned it in kind. And he tried to fit in. His legs got sore as he tried to regain his best shape fast. His mind got tired as he tried to absorb all the new information being fed him by the coaches and in the playbook.

He pulled on his scarlet-red, royal-blue, and white Buffalo uniform with the red buffalo on the white helmet for the first time in Detroit. He did not start. Six minutes into the game he was sent in. He went out for a pass. He was open in the end zone. Haven Moses was open in the opposite corner. Tom Flores threw a touchdown pass to Moses.

Simpson did not return until the fourth quarter. He fidgeted on the bench while some fans chanted, "We want Simpson." Finally, he went back in. He ran at guard for 1 yard. He ran a pitchout for 1 yard. He ran pass patterns, but the ball was not thrown to him. Finally, on a sweep right, he found a hole, slipped through it, and went for 14 yards. He blocked a blitzing linebacker as Harris threw a touchdown pass to Enyart.

Detroit won the game, 14–12, and in the locker room, the reporters crowded around O.J. He said, "It's never good to lose, but I'm glad I've got a game behind me. Was I bothered by the pressure? Well, publicity creates pressure. But publicity is good for the team and good for the league and what's good for them is good for me. I didn't play much, but I'm tired because I haven't practiced much. I'll be ready when the real season is."

He remained concerned about his new hometown. "I guess in the winter when it snows you people stay inside all the time," he said to a secretary in the office during the week. Hadn't he ever been in snow? she wondered. He said, "I've been in the snow. In and out, quick."

It was not snowing when he debuted in his hometown, luring a crowd of 45,070. He played about half the game. He ran five times for 25 yards, returned two kickoffs for 35 yards, and caught two passes for 7 yards. Baltimore, led by John Unitas, breezed, 20–7.

In Cleveland, in the opening game of the annual preseason doubleheader there, the Bills lost to Chicago, 23–16. Simpson ran well with kickoffs and passes, but he rushed for only 8 yards. He almost broke one for a touchdown, but was barely knocked down after returning a kickoff 47 yards.

In Los Angeles, he had his own homecoming in the Coliseum as his new team faced the Rams in the final exhibition game. Psyched-up, Simpson ran a kickoff back 85 yards for a touchdown, but it was ruled he had stepped out of bounds after only 41 yards. However, he gained only 20 yards on seven carries. Two passes were aimed at him. One was overthrown. He dropped the other. The Rams routed the Bills, 50–20. Ram coach Allen admitted, "My players were inspired to stop the rookie superstar." Deacon Jones growled, "Weren't no rookie going to make me look bad."

Afterwards, Simpson was a depressed young man.

"The season is ready, but I'm not sure I am," he admitted. "I'm just getting in shape. I haven't been run enough in games to get going. And I'm having a lot of trouble mastering my running routes and pass patterns. It's not just a matter of learning the basic plays. That's easy. But they have so many varieties on each one that it's confusing. I have to learn about one hundred different pass routes, for example. And when they audibilize a different play at the line of scrimmage I'm sometimes confused as to my assignment.

"The running is different, too. At USC I was allowed to look for a hole. Here, I have a definite hole to hit, whether it's open or not. The players' and coaches' attitude is different, too. In college it was rah-rah. Everyone was excited. I enjoyed it. It stirred me up. Here, it's more relaxed. Everyone has a job to do and he's expected to do it. No matter what you do, coach Rauch isn't going to tell you you did good. You have to get yourself up."

Rauch said, "He'll be all right. It takes time. When we drafted him number one, we obviously respected him. After working with him a few weeks, the respect is even greater now. He's doing a good job of curtailing his appearances and keeping his mind in football. A lot of people have been requesting his time, but he's level-headed and handles it well. People don't seem to get on his nerves. Obviously he has more pressure on him than the average rookie. It's a tougher league than most people realize. He won't find it easy. But I think he'll make it."

Bills' owner Wilson said, "He's going to be sensational. I can't tell you how excited I am about him."

The Bills opened at home against the New York Jets and a record crowd of more than 45,000 filled their old stadium. They showed up with straw hats with blue ribbons adorned with "All the Way with O.J." They yelled expectantly every time he touched the ball.

He returned the opening kickoff 25 yards. Swiftly, he turned end for 22 yards. He sped with a screen pass 55 yards, breaking two tackles. In the third quarter, he turned end, cut inside three tacklers and carried one over as he went 8 yards for his first pro touchdown. But he wound up running only ten times and gaining only 35 yards on his rushes.

Joe Namath directed a Jet attack that took off at the finish for a 33–19 triumph. As the gun sounded, Simpson rushed across the field to shake Namath's hand, congratulating him. To his surprise, Namath held onto his hand for an extra few seconds and praised him in return.

Later, Jet coach Weeb Ewbank said, "He scared us every time he had the ball." Simpson sighed and said, "I didn't have the ball much."

Houston came to town. More than 40,000 turned out. Simpson carried just nineteen times for only 58 yards. His longest run was a 6-yarder. Houston threw Kemp for losses six times and intercepted him three times and ex-Trojan Pete Beathard led the Oilers to a 17–3 victory. Buffalo's losing streak stretched to twelve over two seasons.

Denver came to town. Again, more than 40,000 turned out. Finally, Simpson broke loose. The Bills ran up a team record of twenty-eight first downs. O.J. either ran or caught a pass for twelve of those. He ran twenty-four times for 110 yards. It was the first time a Bill ballcarrier had run for 100 or more yards in three years. He also caught five passes for 45 yards. Jack Kemp passed for 249 yards. The Bills rolled up 406 yards, their most in three years. They came from behind to outscore the Broncos, 41–28, to break their losing streak.

Simpson's longest run was 28 yards, but he slashed for 10, 12, 14 yards here and there, breaking tackles and making the yards that controlled the ball. He said later, "It was a relief to have a good game and get back on a winning side. I ran well. I also feel I blocked well. We played well." Rauch said, "I wasn't that impressed with his yardage. I know he's capable of that and more. It was good to see him showing the other side of a complete player—good blocking."

Saban, the Denver coach, who used to be the Buffalo coach, said, "Simpson sure keeps you loose at all times. He's very dangerous." Floyd Little, the great Denver runner, said, "Simpson looked outstanding, but it usually takes a year or two for a runner to find himself in this league and I'm not surprised he's had his troubles." Simpson said, "After today, I don't think I should have any more trouble."

But that day it was Denver. The next Sunday it was Houston in the Astrodome. Simpson ran thirteen times and could only gain 27 yards. He caught three passes for 32 yards. Catching a pass, he was crashed into a backflip and stunned. Kemp was intercepted four times. The Oilers swept the Bills, 28–14. Larry Felser wrote in the Buffalo *Evening News* that inferior blocking by the Bills' mediocre offensive line was depriving

Simpson of a chance to shine, and foiling the team's entire ground game.

Simpson had suffered a concussion hitting his head on the hard Astroturf and doctors insisted he sit out the following week's game at home against Boston. Wayne Patrick took over for O.J. and ran for 131 yards as Boston was beaten, 23–16.

O.J. returned the following Sunday against a tougher foe, the Raiders at Oakland. He carried six times for 50 yards. But ex-Bill Daryle Lamonica threw six times for touchdowns in the first half. The Raiders completely outclassed the Bills, 50–21. To add insult to injury, quarterback Jim Harris was hit hard and suffered torn knee ligaments which sould sideline him for the season.

Trying to become the first top Black quarterback, Harris was really jolted by his injury. So were Simpson and other Blacks on the team who were rooting for Jim. Now, Kemp, a player past his prime, a person looking to politics for his future, had to carry most of the load, with young Dan Darragh moving in as the reserve.

In Miami, the Bills had the ball inside the Dolphin 10 four times in the first thirty-five minutes and settled for two field goals. They wound up losing, 24–7. This was not Don Shula's Dolphins who would become a power a few years later, but George Wilson's woeful crew which would win only three games all season. Simpson caught four passes for 60 yards but ran only ten times for just 12 yards. He kept butting his head into a stone wall. It was a sad situation.

Afterward, he sat by his locker. Blood coagulated at

the bridge of his nose. His right hand showed a slash. He said, "We get behind so fast we have to throw and never get to run much. I saw a lot of old Nick Buoniconti today. He was after me, my friend. He is some linebacker. Generally, I've been surprised pros haven't hit me as hard as collegians, but Buoniconti hit me hard. Losing is new to me. I lost four games the last four years. I lost five now in the last seven weeks. I really thought it'd be getting better by now."

It was midseason. Rauch growled, "We're losing as a team. Some individuals are playing poorly. I'm not blaming Simspon, but it would have helped him help us if he'd reported on time." Felser wrote, "Some of O.J.'s troubles are of his own making. He has blown a lot of assignments and too often his pass patterns lack any semblance of precision. But it still must be conceded that the chief reason for his lack of success is that the Bills are giving him the kind of holes no self-respecting moth would take credit for. Most of the time, two or three tacklers greet him at the line of scrimmage."

Simpson admitted, "I need help I'm not getting. I'm not running the ball enough. And when I get it I'm not free to do my thing. The best of backs need running room and I'm getting crowded. The team needs help. There's talent here, but weaknesses, too. We're not one of the stronger teams. The coach is smart, but he has lost contact with the players. Of course, doing poorly sets everyone on edge. I didn't expect a lot, but I guess I hoped for the best and I'm disappointed."

13 A Rough Road

He was leading a difficult life, making appearances on Monday, serving the team the rest of the week. "One Monday it was New York for a picture layout in a magazine, next it was Detroit to make a commercial, then New York again for an interview with ABC. Even at home, if I can now call Buffalo home, it's hectic. I get thirty to thirty-five pieces of fan mail a day. I sign a couple of hundred autographs a day.

"I'll never forget when I was a boy and turned down by Stan Musial and Ernie Banks. And Ernie is my mother's first cousin, though he didn't know me. I vowed I'd sign if I ever got the chance. But the kids even come knocking at the door just when we've got the baby to sleep. I don't go out to eat or go out shopping much because I'm mobbed . . . unless I wear my old jeans and tennis shoes and go out needing a shave so people will look right past me.

"Buffalo isn't too bad. The people are terrific fans. I don't think they have as many other interests and they're really behind the team even though the team isn't doing well. There isn't that much to do here, which is all right. This way, I'm home more with my wife and daughter. We've made friends with the older people in our building. In L.A. most of our friends were young people connected with the SC football team."

After one early game a Buffalo sportswriter had gotten Simpson aside and asked him to compare Buffalo with other cities he'd known. Simpson said little about Buffalo, but praised other cities. When the story appeared, many local citizens were upset. The team publicist phoned Barnes to ask his help in straightening out the situation. Barnes suggested he might get Simpson on a national television show where O.J. could praise his new city to the skies. He landed him an appearance on the Merv Griffin talkathon. Mike Garrett was booked, too.

Asked about Buffalo, O.J. said, "It's a great place. Greatest fans in the world. I hope all this talk about moving the franchise to another city is wrong."

Surprised, Garrett said, "O.J., O.J. Are you feeling all right? Tell me this: Would you rather play in Buffalo or Anaheim Stadium?"

"Mike," Simpson confessed, "anywhere but Buffalo I'd play for nothing."

However, he made up for his revolt against the town in other ways. Publicist Jack Horrigan pointed out some examples: "One time O.J. was dispatched to a bank in Buffalo to hand out autographed copies of the team yearbook. To save time we had O.J.'s signature stamped in them ahead of time. But the very first kid in line complained he wanted to see O.J. sign his own signature. So O.J. signed about a thousand. And wound up posing for pictures.

"He's always the last man out of the dressing room. And once he's out he's always set upon by the kids and he always stands and signs for them so he's always the last man in the team bus, too. In Miami there must have been a million kids around him and nine out of ten were white kids. Color doesn't count when it comes to Simpson. He's special."

O.J. got a letter from the teacher of a ten-year-old boy from Rochester, Ronald Ryhal, who had a face full of freckles and a problem with pals who teased him endlessly about them. They told him nobody with freckles had ever become a good athlete. He believed them. The teacher told him, "A lot of people have freckles." He said, "Yes, but no football players have freckles."

She wrote that she herself knew the names of only two football players—Joe Namath and O.J. Simpson—and since Simpson played for the nearby Buffalo Bills, she was writing him to ask if he would write Ronald. Only O.J. had no freckles—none that showed, anyway. So he turned the note over to Jack Kemp, who had his share. And Jack wrote Ronald:

DEAR RONNIE:
O.J. Simpson asked me to write because he heard you didn't believe any professional football players have freckles. I do and I have played pro football for 13 years. So do several other players I know. You must learn, as so many people have, that it isn't the color of your skin or what you look like that matters in life. What really matters is what kind of a boy you are.
Be grateful you have this opportunity to rise above a problem, because every problem we conquer the better we become. Set yourself a goal and let nothing

keep you from it. People don't like you for your face. They like you for what's inside—your honesty, courage, determination and other good qualities.

Well, be good, try hard and learn to laugh.

Your friend, Jack Kemp.

After the Miami game, the team had met and decided what it needed was more parties. A Halloween party was scheduled. Coach Rauch decided what was needed was less Kemp and he went with young Darragh at home against Kansas City but all he got out of it was a 24–7 defeat, sixth loss for the Bills in eight outings. Of course KC was a vastly superior team so it was no surprise. O.J. ran sixteen times for 41 yards.

The games were beginning to melt into each other. With the season shot, practices were tedious and there was a lot of tenseness among the players, who blamed each other for their situation. In New York, in rain and mud, first Darragh, then Kemp were KO'd physically and end Briscoe, a former quarterback, came in during a 16–6 loss to the Jets. O.J. jarred the Jets some, running fourteen times for 70 yards and having a touchdown called back because he had moved toward the line of scrimmage before the snap and was penalized for having been in motion.

Jimmy Cannon wrote: "New York and the wind threw rain-bloated clouds around the dirty sky above Shea Stadium. The field where the Jets beat Buffalo in a boring football game was a swamp. The players were clad in mud. The football was greasy in their wet hands. The puddles they fell into were filthy. But all

Sundays have been miserable for O.J. Simpson in the American League.

"It was beautiful when O.J. played football on Saturdays. He would run in his hunched, arm-swinging way behind Mike Taylor or Ron Yary. They would cut down the other people and there was daylight for O.J. to run to on Saturday. But the night seems to sweep across the field fast as tacklers darken the afternoon on Sunday.

"The Bills are a bad team and they betrayed O.J. again. He has worked with four quarterbacks this season and this turns a team into a confused rabble. The Sundays can't be competent if O.J. earns his money. They have to be spectacular or he is a failure. He ran better than any one on either team but that isn't enough.

"The Jets respect him. 'He played hard football,' explained Gerry Philbin, the great New York end. 'He was overanxious, trying too hard.' A reporter said, 'On pass blocking, you get around him pretty easy.' Philbin said, 'He isn't known for his pass blocking.'

"The Jets figured they handled O.J. because they held him under a hundred yards. 'It has to come,' one after another said. 'O.J. is great,' Verlon Biggs said. Coach Weeb Ewbank said, 'I told them they could wind up with a handful of air if they tried to tackle him alone. I told them to gang-tackle him. It was hard to run on the field, but he did pretty good.'

"The sad Saturdays hadn't soured O.J. Afterwards, he sat on a stool in his locker and praised a team that had fallen apart on him. It wasn't a guy trying to improve a situation with con. He made it clear that this was a team and he was a part of it. He had the dignity of a winner as he made polite replies even to mean questions.

" 'You down?' a guy wanted to know.

" 'No,' he said. 'I feel I can do as well as any runningback with what I've got to work with. But if I go out there every Sunday and get beat up, you might as well win.' "

Back in Buffalo, the Bills won, 28–3 over Miami. Simpson sparked the victory with his finest performance as a pro. He opened the game with a 73-yard kickoff return, scored twice on 55-yard and 8-yard passes from Jack Kemp, caught three passes for 81 yards, and ran twenty-one times for 72 yards.

But a week later, in New England, the Bills bowed to Boston, 35–21. And Simpson was surpassed by Carl Garrett in a duel between Rookie of the Year candidates. O.J. ran seventeen times for 98 yards, including a 25-yarder. Garrett ran thirteen times for 96 yards. But Garrett also had a 62-yard kickoff return, set up one score with a 40-yard punt return and scored the last touchdown on a 44-yard run. The crowd of 25,584 chanted "O.J. Who?" at the end of the game. Simpson accepted it good-naturedly, stopping among them to sign autographs.

He had hit hard, knocking tough Patriot linebacker John Bramlett unconscious in a collision at the sidelines.

The next week he carried only thirteen times for only 35 yards in a Buffalo blizzard, but the Bills did beat Cincinnati 16–13. In freezing weather, the Bengals lost seven fumbles and the game. O.J. fumbled once, losing a touchdown at the goal line. It was the worst weather for a football game in the memory of the observers. The writers termed it an "Arctic survival test." Afterward Simpson shivered and said, "I'll tell you, it isn't southern California.

"I've never played in anything close to conditions like this. I never want to play in them again. I guess this was expected when I came here but I never expected this. They say you should experience everything once, but this one thing I could have gone without."

Later, after the season, he laughed and said, "To tell you the truth, in December, when the offense came off the field, I wouldn't sit near the linemen. The people threw snowballs at them. I didn't want to get hit."

In Kansas City, in the next-to-last game of the season, it was merely very cold. O.J. ran for 62 yards in only eleven carries. He had his longest run of the year, a 32-yarder, to tie the game at 19–19 with eight minutes left. It was a spectacular run in which he danced by tacklers, then ran right over two into the end zone. But Jan Stenerud kicked his fifth field goal with two minutes to play to beat the Bills, 22–19.

The finale was in sunny San Diego, which Simpson felt was fortunate because it would put him in a position to get home fast. The last game, leaving the Bills at four victories and ten defeats for the season, was a travesty, a 45–6 loss to the Chargers. Simpson was given the ball just seven times and he ran for just 27 yards.

Finally it was finished and he just got out of there as fast as he could and headed home to his new $100,000 home in the Bel Air Sky Crest sector of Beverly Hills, off Mulholland Drive, and he went out into the sunshine and took a fast swim in his 40-foot pool.

Added up, his first pro year had not been too bad. He had run 181 times for 697 yards in thirteen games. This placed him sixth in rushing in his league. He had caught thirty passes for 343 yards. He had returned twenty-one kickoffs for 529 yards. His total offense of 1,560 yards was impressive. He outgained Garrett, but lost Rookie of the Year honors to him. But O.J. had rushed the ball twenty or more times only in two games all season. He had run ten or less times four games. And he had fallen far below what had been hoped from him.

He sat in his den amid his trophies and pictures of his greatest exploits, which hung on the wood-paneled walls, and he said, "I was not as good a professional player as I had hoped to be. A lot entered into it. I got a late start. And I didn't get as much help as I was used to getting. But on the other hand I didn't help my team as much as I usually do. I didn't master all my plays and pass-patterns. It was more complicated than I expected. I made more mistakes than I should have. And then I rarely got a chance to unwind by running a lot.

"It was a frustrating experience. Frustrating because we lost so much. And frustrating because we passed so much. I believe we would have done better if we had run more, extablished a running game to go with our passing game. I know I would have done better and been able to give the team more if I had been run more. Most of my runs were when the other team was expecting a run. I'm used to being beat and tired after a game. It was frustrating to feel fresh after losses with a lot left in me I'd never gotten a chance to give.

"I had a problem in that by reporting late I got very little scrimmaging with my offensive line. This is important. The blockers have to know how a back runs. I run different than a lot of backs and my blockers didn't know my ways. The coach thought I turned my sweeps up field too quick. Trying to do it his way, trying to stretch it out and run wider, I got fouled up. I'm sorry, but I have to run my way. I've learned that. And I'm going back to my way, to the quick cuts.

"The coach was critical of me, even sarcastic. That's his right. I know I did not do as well as he expected. But I respond better to a pat on the back than to a boot in the rear. He does a lot of yelling. The players don't pay much attention to yelling. I was surprised by the players' attitude. They took losing too easy. At SC we wanted to cut our throats when we lost. But I guess when you play twice as many games and play for years and years you start to take the games in stride, win or lose.

"There was a lot of division on our team between the older players and the younger players. The older guys were living in the past. They were always talking about championships we didn't share in. They're on the way out and they weren't worried about now, the way the young players were. The young players were worried about winning jobs. There was a lot of every man for himself and not much pulling together for the team.

"Professional football is much more different than college football than I thought it would be. Playing for your jobs and for money makes it a new game. It stops being sport and becomes a business. The guys are supporting families and concerned about their futures. It was hard to endure the fringe players who were really worried about keeping their place all the time. Making friends and then seeing the guys cut was terrible. Suddenly, for most of them, football was finished. If you're cut from a bottom team, it's usually the end of the line. Seeing veterans reach the end of the line and get released was a rough thing, too.

"I guess it matured me. The game stopped being fun. I still like to play but now I know I have to get myself up. I missed some of Marv Goux's pep talks and the rah-rah spirit. Maybe if we'd been on a winner we'd have had better spirit. We need a leader. I think a lot of guys expected me to take over, but I'm not a cheerleader type. I'm quiet and I try to do my job. Maybe I can lead by example. Anyway, being a rookie you can't say a lot of the things to the guys and to the coach you feel. And coming in late with all the publicity I had about my money I was just trying to be one of the guys and to fit in.

"I learned a lot and I think I'll benefit from the experience," Simpson concluded.

In Buffalo, Johnny Rauch said, "O.J. made more mistakes than I'd have liked him to make. When you think of O.J. you think of him being the greatest and he didn't meet the standard and certainly has the ability to be better." But one of his offensive linemen, Joe O'Donnell, said, "I feel badly that we weren't able to do a better job of blocking for him. He has ways of running we have to get used to. He likes to cut back into the middle after starting quickly and we have to learn to anticipate. What he made, he made on his own most of the time. If O.J. is going to do what he can do, it's got to be because we have a team that will be able to help him do it."

In May, Marguerite presented O.J. with the son he so much wanted. They named him Jason. Later in the spring, O.J. appeared at the New York Coliseum, representing Chevrolet at the auto show. Impeccably barbered and tailored, he was resplendent in blue blazer with silver buttons, tight gray slacks and a dark blue shirt with a mod print tie. "Hiya there. How are you? How have you been?" he was saying to people he never met. Writer John Devaney observed, "There is a genuine friendliness to O.J. He obviously likes people."

Pressed on his play as a first-year pro and the disappointments and criticisms, Simpson answered the questions straight out, honestly, unafraid, articulately. He said, "Look, they didn't set up anything special for me. If that's the system, all right. But I can't be their big back if I'm just given the ball on ordinary plays and only twelve or thirteen times a game. So I'll have to concentrate on my pass receiving more and work at being a better blocker and hope they open things up for me."

Wistfully he smiled. He said, "I don't think I was spoiled by my money. I'm not the fat-cat type. I have too much pride. I want too much to be the best. But I didn't feel inspired. I lacked the killer instinct. I don't think I was distracted by my outside interests too much. I only worked at them on Mondays when everyone did their own things. But maybe the traveling took something out of me. And it worried me to find myself worried about this thing or that thing, about things that weren't football things, during football season.

He concluded, "I'm going to concentrate more on football this next season, try to get myself going more, try to get more with the team. We had a new coach, a new system, and a lot of new players. We won three more games than the team had won the year before and we came close to winning a few more. This new season things should get a lot better."

14 It Takes Time

There was no real reason to assume things would get better with the Bills in Buffalo. There was no real reason for O.J. Simpson to assume they would get better for him there. And they didn't—not for a couple of more years. Oh, they started to get better in his second season in pro ball, but then suddenly it went worse.

The Bills lost five out of six exhibition games prior to the regular season in 1970. They had added a few rookies, notably a sharp passer from San Diego State, Dennis Shaw; a dangerous runner from UCLA, Greg Jones; and a tough defensive lineman, O.J.'s old pal from San Francisco and USC, Al Cowlings, but the team effort remained erratic.

Asked if he wanted to say some controversial things about the situation, O.J. smiled and said, "No, no. When you play with a team like Buffalo, you don't get people mad at you. You need all the friends you can get."

Shaw soon won the starting role. Kemp had quit to enter politics and he wound up in Washington. Darragh remained the backup. Harris was busted to the taxi squad, which depressed Simpson, who had wanted to see Jim make it as the first top Black quarterback. "It was sort of a crusade," O.J. admitted. "But while he has the talent, he may lack the personality. A quarterback has to lead and take charge in the huddle. Jim is quiet and he just won't talk up. Shaw sure is cockier."

In the opener, at home against Denver, Darragh and Shaw between them completed only ten passes for less than 100 yards. Simpson ran only eighteen times for just 49 yards. He returned a kickoff for 31 yards and caught three passes for 49 yards, but otherwise the day was a total loss. The Bills lost to the Broncos, 25–10, and almost 35,000 fans went away disappointed. In the second game, at home against Los Angeles, Darragh and Shaw threw for 172 yards, but Simpson gained only 24 yards on fourteen carries and didn't catch a pass or return a kick and the Rams breezed, 19–0, and more than 46,000 fans were let down again.

As New York's Jets arrived, the big-city writers bore in on O.J. Simpson remained the subject of most of the advance stories. He sighed and said, "I had a good preseason, but I'm off to a poor start in the regular season. I've been lucky everywhere I go. I'm always billed as the coming attraction and people are still making excuses for me. The writers never say that I had a bad game. They blame it on the team. I appreciate that, but it isn't fair to the team."

Stirred up, he took the second kickoff 95 yards to a touchdown. He fumbled it at first, but picked it up, tore through a pack of tacklers, broke free, and spread the distance. Later, he noted, "I ran back two kickoffs for touchdowns in college and now one in pro and it's funny but I fumbled every one. Maybe fumbling at first throws the rushers off-stride and breaks up the field for you. Maybe it makes them let down and gives you a little edge. I'd fumbled the first one today and didn't run it back. After fumbling the second one, I heard the crowd start to boo, it fired me up, and I picked it up and ran it."

After that, he ran back another kickoff 46 yards, caught three passes for 63 yards, and rushed twenty-one times for 99 yards. Shaw passed for 317 yards, mostly to Briscoe and Moses. Between them they put on a spectacular show. Joe Namath passed for two touchdowns and Jim Turner kicked five field goals, but late in the game Shaw threw 25 yards to Briscoe to put the Bills ahead 34–31 and they hung on for a rare upset.

Losing coach Weeb Ewbank, obviously disappointed, conceded, "If the forty-six thousand Buffalo fans who were here today had been waiting to see the real O.J. they saw him today. He's improved in every department and he's the same great runner he's ever been but he just hasn't been able to show it for lack of blocking. He's a threat to go all the way every time he touches the ball. He's the kind of guy who can start to his left, turn around, and go back to the right and go for a touchdown. With Shaw, the Bills have the making of an offense."

Jet linebacker Larry Grantham said, "Shaw is going to be great, but I think O.J. has the potential to be the best back to ever play the game. He didn't get much help last year. No runner can run around or over everyone. But give him a hole or a broken field and he is gone. You have to watch him every minute his side has the ball. He can break a game wide open. His scoring runback was sensational and threw us off stride."

Simpson said, "It was our best day. I hope there will be a lot more like it now."

There were not. In Pittsburgh, the Bills fell right back and were dropped, 23–10. The Steelers kicked off away from Simpson and keyed on him. He was held to 60 yards on fourteen carries and didn't catch a pass. Shaw threw for 201 yards, but it wasn't enough. Back home the following Sunday, the Bills were bombed by Miami, 33–14. Simpson returned a couple of kickoffs 90 yards, but rushed only eleven times for 35 yards and caught only three passes for 24 yards. Shaw threw for 348 yards, but without the balance of a running game, the Bills still were easily stopped when it counted.

The local writers reported that it was silly that Simpson wasn't used more, but Rauch remained unmoved. Simpson seemed depressed. And lonely. Not liking Buffalo, his wife had taken the kids back to L.A. and he was living alone.

In Shea Stadium, the Jets kicked away from Simpson, and he settled for 55 yards on fourteen rushes, and Shaw threw for only 163 yards. But in a dreary game the Bills sprung an uninspired upset, 10–6. Then in Boston, Simpson surged to spark a spectacular 45–10 upset of the Patriots. He was given the ball only seventeen times, but gained 123 yards, including a fantastic 56-yard run from scrimmage that broke the game wide open in the second period.

It was up and down, up and down, like riding a roller coaster, Simpson sighed later.

The following week he was down. And out for the season. He had run ten times for 40 yards in the first half, scored a touchdown, and had kept the Bills in contention with Cincinnati when, returning a kickoff just before intermission, he was hit hard by a series of tacklers and wound up collapsed in a pile of pain. Dr. Joseph Godfrey, the team physician, determined he had suffered a tear of the capsule behind his left knee, and said he would probably need surgery and definitely be sidelined for the season.

This was November the eighth, the eighth game of the season for the Bills, and without Simpson they were put to rout in the second half to lose to the Bengals, 43–14. O.J. said, "They had stopped kicking to me so we used a trick return. I lined up on the right and ran all the way across the field to the left to take the ball. Going up the sidelines, I got hit and couldn't pull away and couldn't fall because a guy was on my legs, and they kept coming and hitting me like I was a dummy punching bag and I had to be carried off the field."

He sat on a table in the dressing room stained and sweating and swearing softly with his knee wrapped up and splinted and paining him and the disappointment was etched deep in his face. He was taken to Buffalo General Hospital for surgery.

He woke up the next morning figuring they'd put him under and taken him and cut during the night. He picked up the newspaper and read a headline, SIMPSON DOESN'T NEED SURGERY. "I thought, 'Idiot press. Can't they get anything right?' But then I started wondering and pulled off the bandage and the splint and there was my whole knee with no cut in it."

They had decided it would repair with rest.

At the time of his injury he had picked up his rushing pace impressively to 488 yards on 120 carries and was third in the league in running and he had run back seven kickoffs for 333 yards and was first in the league in this department and caught ten passes for 139 yards, so in little more than half a season he had gained nearly 1,000 yards in total offense. He had an astonishing 48-yard average in kickoff returns, which showed what he could do given a broken field. But he was through for the year. And he went home to Los Angeles.

Without him, the Bills did not win another game. Shaw wound up throwing for 2,507 yards and wound up with the Rookie of the Year laurel Simpson had lost and Briscoe caught for 1,036 yards, but without a rusher, the Bills could not contain their foes and they tied Baltimore, but were beaten by Baltimore and by Boston and by the Giants and put to rout by Chicago and by Miami, the latter by 45–7 in the finale. Their running was so poor no one even was able to catch O.J. for the team lead in the last six games while he sat in the sun in southern California.

The knee healed. Early in the summer, Simpson and some other Bills who lived on the West Coast, including quarterback Shaw, got together and agreed to quit complaining about Buffalo and about head coach Rauch. There were rumors of the franchise shifting to Seattle, of trades, of a change in coaches, but O.J. and the others were tired of such talk, which never seemed to be translated into action. They decided this was their lot in life and they should begin to make the most of it.

Just as the team arrived at Niagara University for preseason training camp, Rauch appeared on a television show and criticized two popular former Bills—one traded and one retired. Angered, owner Wilson said he was going to make a statement defending them. Rauch said, "If you do that, get yourself another coach." In his past two seasons, Ruach's teams had lost twenty of twenty-eight games. Wilson took this into consideration.

That afternoon Simpson ran into Harvey Johnson, the Bills' director of player personnel. "Uncle Harvey, how you doing, man?" asked O.J.

"I am now the coach," said Johnson. "And we now have a new offense. It is called O.J. left, O.J. right, and, occasionally, O.J. up the middle."

Simpson had grown a new mustache, which Rauch would never have permitted. It was a Fu Manchu job which dripped to his chin.

"What are you doing with that hair on your face?" the new coach asked.

"My wife likes it," O.J. said.

"Don't fumble," Johnson said.

Under Johnson, the Bills began to rebuild again. Most of the heroes of the past had departed and the remaining youngsters took to his light touch. Simpson said, "Let's face it, I hated Rauch. I thought he used me wrong. I thought he ran our offense wrong. And I thought he was cold. The new coach is more easygoing and understanding. He'll discipline you, but with a smile." And under Johnson, the Bills split six exhibition games. But the preseason is the preseason and the results are meaningless because try as they may the players do not play as they do in the regular season.

Simpson now had to run behind an extremely inexperienced blocking line consisting of rookies Willie Young and Donnie Green at tackles and Bruce Jarvis at center and second-year men John Reilly and Rich Cheek at guards.

In the opening game, at home, Johnson tried to instill confidence into his offensive unit. Early in the game, the Bills drove deep into Dallas territory. Failing to make a first down on a third down, they were faced with a field-goal situation at the 6. Shaw and O.J. signaled to the sidelines not to send in the field-goal unit.

Johnson said later, "I decided that these guys needed a lift, a vote of confidence. It wasn't that O.J. and Dennis were running the club, as people have said. I just went along with them."

O.J. got the call from Shaw and went squirming through the Doomsday Defense of Dallas for 6 yards and the touchdown. But he ran thirteen other times for only 19 more yards. Shaw passed for 353 yards, but it wasn't enough and he wasn't to have another game like it all year. Dallas, bound for the championship at season's end, won a high-scoring contest, 49-37.

The next week, Miami came in and belted the Bills, 29-14, although Simpson ran nine times for 82 yards and uncorked a 46-yard scoring jaunt. The next week at Minnesota the Purple Gang and other defenders of the Vikings shut off Shaw and held Simpson to 45 yards in twelve carries and breezed, 19-0. Back home the week after that, Shaw was so ineffective he was replaced by Harris, up from the Taxi squad for a last shot, and Simpson actually lost 10 yards in seven carries and Baltimore blasted the Bills, 43–0.

Shaw had passed for less than 100 yards total in the last two games and Simpson was getting nowhere running without room to run and the defense had deteriorated and suddenly it was the same old story again and a wave of depression swept over the Bills. After four weeks of his third season, Simpson saw matters getting worse, not better. In New York, he carried one kickoff back for 43 yards and rushed eighteen times for 69 yards, but Shaw was still struggling and the Jets jumped on them, 28–17.

In San Diego the following Sunday, Simpson slashed eighteen times for 106 yards while Shaw completed four passes for 20 yards and Harris completed four passes for 36 yards and after the Chargers had breezed, 20–3, Sid Gillman said, "What a shame that Simpson has to be stuck with that team." Back home, O.J. ran sixteen times for 42 yards and caught two passes for 42 more yards and Shaw had a 220-yard day passing, but two touchdowns in the last quarter, the last one a 61-yard punt return in the last two minutes, salvaged a 28–23 victory for St. Louis.

So the Bills were winless at midseason. Simpson was sixth in rushing in the league, but he observed, "I see films of the runners who are running for the top teams behind the big blocking lines and I think I'm better than they are, to tell you the truth, and I wonder how I would do on their teams and how they would do on mine. It hurts me watching Norm Bulaich and Larry Csonka on TV getting a lot of yardage for Baltimore and Miami. Sometimes I wish I was in their situation.

You can't run when there's no place to go. And losing game after game after game has to get to you. But this is my team and I'm as responsible for the losing as anyone, so I guess we'll just have to tough it out and hope for improvement."

It didn't come in Miami, where the Bills were put to rout by 34–0, although Simpson ran ten times for an astonishing 90 yards and outgained Csonka. Incredibly, he still was being used sparingly, but he had stopped talking about it because there was nothing he could do about it, and, for all his preseason talk of building his offense around Simpson, Johnson wasn't doing it. He went all the way with Harris in this one and it didn't help.

In New England, Simpson ran sixteen times for 61 yards, but Harris had a difficult day and Jim Plunkett, headed for Rookie of the Year honors, passed the Patroits to a 38–33 triumph in a wide-open game. Back home, O.J. ran fourteen times for 48 yards, Shaw and Harris split the passing ineffectively and the Jets triumphed, 20–7 to leave the Bills 0–9.

At home against New England, a team which really wasn't much better than them, Buffalo had a shot at a victory and they shot the works. Simpson carried a couple of kickoffs back 57 yards and ran fourteen times for 61 yards, including a slicing, 7-yard scoring run that was exciting, and the Bills finally broke into the victory column, 27–20. Shaw had only a fair day, but Plunkett was no better.

In Baltimore, it was back to the beaten track, 24–0, as Simpson was held to 26 yards in nine carries and Shaw was choked off. At home against Houston, less than 30,000 fans turned out, and the Oilers won, 20–14, on a late drive and a score with twenty-four seconds to play. Simpson rushed twelve times for only 29 yards, but he did have a sizzling short 6-yard scoring run that put the Bills back in the game in the fourth quarter. Shaw had a hot hand, completing twenty passes for 233 yards, but it wasn't enough.

Which brought the Bills down to the season finale in Kansas City, where the Chiefs chopped them up at 22–9 to leave them at 1–13, which had been their record when they drafted O.J. four years before. Simpson ran fourteen times for 68 yards, then ran for a 5:55 plane and a fast flight home to southern California.

He had rushed 183 times for 742 yards, which wasn't too bad, seventh-best in his circuit, but still was less by far than he was capable of doing, but didn't do, partly because he averaged only thirteen carries a game, partly because in his carries he didn't see any daylight. His team was the worst in football. Shaw had slipped to 1,800 yards passing, Briscoe to 600 yards receiving. Heralded rookie receiver J.D. Hill played little.

Simpson had caught twenty-one passes for 162 yards and run back fourteen kickoffs for 107 yards, giving him a total offense of more than 1,000 yards, but Buffalo obviously hadn't used him as much as it might have. Other teams were interested in trading for him and there was talk he'd play out his option year and try to jump somewhere else.

The Rams put together a package of players in a bid for him. Many of the players who were possible parts of this package—Deacon Jones, Kermit Alexander, Larry Smith and others—either were traded or sold or dropped or not regulars the next season, but the deal fell through. Which was sad because no one now would know what O.J. might have done with a top team, nor what pennants or play-off victories he might have provided a top team bold enough to deal freely for him.

There were rumors Dallas would deal for Simpson, but it did not. Cal Hill, another Sports Headliners client, another great runner, and a former NFL rushing champion, told Bruce Barnes, Chuck's brother, "O.J. might be a better runner than Jim Brown ever was. If O.J. is with Dallas, I become a better runner and O.J. runs wild. With Dallas he'd be blocked free and in broken fields would run up tremendous yardage totals. With Buffalo, he's the only runner foes have to worry about, he gets little blocking and he has to struggle for every inch."

Barnes observed that Simpson had earned about $180,000 in salary and endorsements in 1971, but business might be going bad. Observed Barnes, "He is tough to sell to ad agencies these days. The agency guys say, 'Simpson, who's he?' O.J.'s still a great name in southern California, but after three years behind Buffalo's weak line he's faded nationally. He needs to restore his image."

Simpson thought about all this through the summer. He said, "Look, the team's been down and losing is terrible. If you're a skier you might like upstate New York and there's nothing that bad about Buffalo, it's just that it's not my kind of city and you live a way of life there that wouldn't be my first choice.

"But, let's face it, after three years, this is my team now. I've been together with a lot of the same guys for a lot of seasons now and we feel togetherness. Losing has driven us together. We've got a good group of cats. We're getting whupped, but we're looking forward to the day when we can win together.

"My wife was with me all season and she made some fast friends and she began to feel more at home in Buffalo. Our real home is in Los Angeles, but if you're an athlete you have a home in the city you're playing for, too, and I can't go on waiting for each season to end, crossing the days off the calendar like a convict.

"I'm not sure what I'll do yet, but I'm not asking to be traded and I've quit thinking about trades that might be made for me, and I'm not thinking right now about making a move on my own. It's a temptation because my career is running out on me, I'm getting beat up, runners don't last long, and I'm not getting anywhere, but I have to start living in the present instead of some fancy future that might never come."

15 Super-Pro at Last

O.J. Simpson sat in the box of the Buffalo owner, Ralph Wilson, at Santa Anita racetrack in Southern California and watched Wilson's horse, West Coast Scout, run last in a stakes race.

Simpson, the owner's guest, smiled and said to Wilson, "This will give you first draft choice at the Keenland Sales."

Wilson laughed. Running last at the racetrack did not entitle him to the top pick at the annual auction of yearling horses as running last in football had brought him the number-one draft choice, Simpson, three seasons before.

Now, as Simpson was about to enter his fourth and final season on his Buffalo Bills' contract and was threatening to play out his option so he could be a free agent and find a place for himself with a better team, Wilson was courting his star in an effort to retain him.

Wilson had some bargaining points. One, Buffalo had come through with a fancy new stadium, which already was under construction and promised to improve the Bills' working conditions considerably. Two, Buffalo had reacquired as coach Lou Saban, who had failed to build a winner in Denver, but was returning to the scene of his greatest success, Buffalo, and who was a coach who believed in a big runner. Even with weak teams at Denver, Floyd Little had been used so extensively by Saban he had become a 1,000-yards-a-season star and a rushing champion. Three, Buffalo had drafted a top rookie offensive lineman, massive Reggie McKenzie from Michigan. Simpson's working conditions figured to be more favorable than before.

Finally, Wilson suggested to Simpson that if he would sign for three more seasons in Buffalo beyond the 1972 campaign, he would be secure to the age of thirty. Argued Wilson, a player who is able to stay put with one organization for a prolonged period enjoys certain benefits. If he needs a friend, he has one. Also, there were no guarantees that he would be able to make a good deal for himself as a free agent. The owners have gentleman's agreements not to steal from one another, and one taking a star has to compensate the loser and runs the risk of giving up more than he gets. Also, a fellow going cold into a new organization and onto a new team, stamped as a transient, would be starting all over again.

Offering a fat new pact estimated at $450,000 for three years, $150,000 a season for 1973, 1974, and 1975, Wilson sold Barnes and Simpson. To everyone's surprise, Simpson signed. He said, "I want to be known as the steady sort. I see athletes jumping teams all around me, especially in pro basketball, and I don't want to get the reputation of being undependable. The money is as good here as it is anywhere else. I've had my troubles here, but management and the players had stuck by me and done right by me and I want to stick with them and do right by them.

"I feel a loyalty to my teammates. We've gone through a lot of dark days together and I want to be with them when we break through to daylight. The new coach and the new system seem promising, but I don't expect miracles anymore. I can't expect to be carried. I feel that with determination I can do more on my own. I think I've grown up a lot. I'm sick and tired of hearing myself grouse about snow and Buffalo. I have a fine home in Los Angeles for off-seasons. I don't think it matters that much where I play in-season. One can be happy anywhere. And the people have treated me marvelously. I owe everyone something and I'm going to start to pay off."

Saban, in his early fifties, had been quarterback and captain of Bo McMillan's marvelous Indiana University teams of the early 1940's. A wartime officer, Saban emerged from service to play pro ball as linebacker and captain of the Cleveland Browns. He became a gypsy coach, moving about in search of a superior situation. He was head coach in college at Case, Northwestern, and Western Illinois. He was head coach in pro ball at Boston before he became the head man in Buffalo. After taking titles in Buffalo, he returned to college ranks to coach Maryland, then departed for Denver. Now he was back in Buffalo.

A stern, tough leader, he was regarded with respect by players. He faced a difficult situation in rebuilding the Bills, who had run through three coaches and several rebuildings in the preceding seasons. He brought in top assistants in Bill Atkins, Stan Jones, Jim Dooley, Ed Cavanaugh, Bob Shaw, and Jim Ringo. Harvey Johnson had reassumed his role as talent chief, aided by Bob Celeri and Elbert Dubenion. Bob Lustig remained the general manager.

They went after linemen in the draft. Walt Patulski, the enormous defensive end from Notre Dame, was the number-one choice, and the brutal blocker, McKenzie, was taken next. Saban was to make some changes. Harris would be cut, which disappointed Simpson, but Jim just didn't seem to have it to be the first top Black quarterback. Shaw reassumed the regular role backed up by veteran Mike Talliaferro. Simpson was promised much more work as the star runner. And he was made co-captain with linebacker Paul Guidry. The team might be improved, but it would not be a big winner and everyone around there knew it. The real goal was to begin to make steady progress.

Simpson was pleased with his progress in the preseason. In one game, he ran twenty-two times for 173 yards, ran 71 yards for one touchdown, and caught an 11-yard pass for another. But in this one, in Chicago, the Bills blew a 24–0 halftime lead and settled for a 24–24 tie at the finish. "Well, we got to get it together as a team," Simpson said. "But I'm getting myself together.

"Saban reminds me of McKay. When he says something, he gives you the impression there's absolutely no way he can be wrong. McKay was the same way. They're not always right, but who is? If they're wrong, you figure maybe you made it that way. After a win he's harder on us than after a loss. He's a perfectionist. He won't accept excuses the way some coaches will. You're sorta afraid of him. I think a player has to be a little afraid of his coach if he's going to give everything he's got. Saban will get it out of you.

"We've got a way to go, but we're getting there. Myself, I don't have any time to spare. This has to be my first big year as a pro. If it is, I'll probably play longer than the five years I set out for myself at first. I look at Saban's history. Under him, Floyd Little led the league in rushing yardage. But he carried the ball at least 100 times a season more than I did. I had slightly higher yards per carry. I think I'll like Saban's ideas. I think I'll get the ball a lot and I think I'll go a long way with it. If I carry the ball twenty times a game, I should gain 1,000 yards. If not, it's my own fault. I'll just have to make the most of what help I do get. I've wasted some seasons. I don't want to waste myself anymore."

Buffalo always had most of its early games at home so it would not have to host teams in its winter weather later on. In 1972, the Bills opened with the first four in its ancient arena. The Jets came in first. And they jolted the Bills, 41–24. Simpson was given the ball only fourteen times and wound up with only 41 yards. He said later, "I was running wild in the exhibition season. I was so happy I was whistling at practice. I haven't done that since I was at USC. Now I'm crying again."

But Saban seemed to see he had made a mistake. He said, "I don't know how our offense can be effective unless we keep giving O.J. the ball. We've figured out several different ways of giving it to him." The next Sunday they gave it to him twenty-nine times and he exploded for 138 yards, his pro high, and the outstanding San Francisco 49ers were stunned, 27–20.

Veteran quarterback John Brodie was blitzed in the first five minutes and walked away with a sprained wrist. Steve Spurrier replaced him and pitched the 49ers to a 20–13 lead midway in the last quarter.

But, Simpson's sizzling runs had kept his club in contention and now Shaw, who had been sputtering, went to work. He hit three passes, one a 25-yarder to Simpson, in a drive that tied it at 20–20. Then an interception gave the ball back to the Bills on the 49er 18. Simpson took it close in three bruising carries and Jim Braxton bucked it over.

The Bills whooped and hollered their upset into the dressing room as the 46,000 fans cheered them off. Sore but smiling, Simpson sat in sweaty disarray in the dressing room and said, "I never had a better time than I had today. I'm as happy about this game as any other game I ever played in. I'm from San Francisco and the 49ers were my favorite team. I used to cheer for these guys. Now I play against them. And I'm happy to have had a part in beating them. The players on this club never quit battling."

The next week was something else again as Baltimore blanked the Bills, 17–0, despite some strong running by Simpson, who only got seventeen carries, but got 78 yards with them. The blocking broke down in front of him and Saban started to shuffle replacements in as Simpson made all sorts of moves, slipping tacklers, for his gains.

He'd get through two and the third tackler would get him. Or he'd get through three and the fourth one would get him. The tacklers kept coming. On one 14-yard run, O.J. broke four tackles and was hit by a fifth. Late in the game he slipped five foes in running 23 yards to the 5, before he was pulled down, but Buffalo failed to score.

But the Bills bounced back to take apart the Patriots, 38–14, the following week as Simpson only ran thirteen times for 31 yards, but got an 11-yard scoring run on one, and completed two passes for 53 yards. This stunned the Pats. On one play, Simpson took the hand-off, faked a run, sucking the defenders in, and threw to Braxton for 19 yards to the New England 17, setting up a touchdown pass from Shaw to Hill. He also connected to former USC end Bob Chandler, another buddy brought in from back home.

On the road for the first time, in Oakland, Simpson was sensational, rushing twenty-eight times for 144 yards, and he almost ran the heavily favored Raiders right out of their Coliseum before Oakland went ahead with less than three minutes to play, 21–16, and then tacked on an insurance score with less than one minute to play to win, 28–16.

It was a strong showing by Buffalo against a much stronger team and most of the writers praised Simpson as the man most responsible. Saban conceded, "He's doing a super job for us." Simpson said, simply, "I'm getting some chances some games."

Even mighty Miami, striving for an undefeated season, was pushed before it prevailed when it played in Buffalo, but Simpson, who had soared to the top of the American Football Conference in rushing, was limited to thirteen carries and gained only 45 yards and the Bills, behind only 16–13 at intermission, could not control the ball in the second half and were defeated at the finish, 30–16.

They went back to giving the ball to Simpson in the seventh game. Given twenty-two chances, he surpassed his previous pro high with 189 yards and almost had many more, although the rising Steelers pulled off a 38–21 victory.

In the third period, Pittsburgh downed a punt on the Buffalo 1, but gave up 5 yards for being offside. From the 6, Simpson took a hand-off from reserve quarterback Taliaferro, ran left, cut back sharply to his right, broke tackles with fierce leg movements, broke free, shifted into high, and sped to the end zone to complete a 94-yard run from scrimmage, longest ever by a Bill, longest in the NFL in thirty years, only 3 yards short of the all-time record.

A few plays later, Buffalo got the ball back deep in its territory again and from the 5, Simpson sliced through the line and cut back and for an instant seemed certain to take off on an even longer run, a 95-yard run, but a linebacker who was virtually blocked into him belted him down. Later it was pointed out that had tight-end Jan White blocked his man outside instead of inside, Simpson almost surely would have gone all the way. With such a run he would have had 272 yards for the day, the all-time pro record.

In any event, he had by midseason proven himself a super-pro just as he had been the class collegian of his era. And he was prominent nationally again and the agency guys wanted him again. Although he had played behind eight different right guards, two left guards, four centers, and three left tackles, and still had gotten the ball less than twenty times in 4 of his side's 7 games, in fact less than fifteen times in 3 games, he had rushed for 666 yards in 136 carries to lead his circuit in rushing. Halfway through the season he had far more than half the yardage he needed for his treasured 1,000-yard year.

At one point Simpson had looked around him in a huddle, laughed, and asked, "Does everyone here know everyone else?" Told this later, Saban confessed, "We don't have an offensive line. We haven't had one since the start of the season. We've used so many different men up front that some of them are strangers to one another and strangers to Simpson and there's no way they can work together or work well with him and what he's gotten, he's gotten on his own. Which is one reason I haven't, as I said I would, used him more. I don't want to waste him or risk getting him hurt. When I can get a good set crew blocking in front of him, I'll use him more and win more with him."

The team was bogged at the bottom again with two victories and five defeats as it turned into the last half of the season, and the players were starting to sag again, but pride in his performance was pushing Simpson on. His handsome face eased into a wistful smile as he assessed the situation: "I remember when Al Cowlings first joined me here and we'd moan and groan every day for the good life in California. Well, there are other guys stuck here, too. And it's not bad. The kids are getting older and getting some personality and they seem to like it better here than in California. There's more room to play. They dig the snow, too.

At twenty-five, I'm getting older, too, and realizing that some things that seemed important just don't make that much difference. What is important is that I make the most of myself in my profession. I'm starting to do that now. I've proven myself as a pro now. But I'll help this team any way I can, carrying forty times a game, or not carrying at all and just blocking. I've cried with these guys, now I'm just waiting for the chance to laugh with them. I want to share champagne with them some day," he said.

It was called "The Year of the Runner." Because of injuries or inconsistencies there was not a single passing quarterback having an outstanding year. But defenses were unable to dominate the game's great running-backs, such as Larry Brown of Washington, Larry Csonka and "Mercury" Morris of Miami, Franco Harris of Pittsburgh, Marv Hubbard of Oakland, Mike Garrett of San Diego, Leroy Kelly of Cleveland, John Riggins of the New York Jets, Ron Johnson of the New York Giants, Calvin Hill of Dallas, John Brockington and MacArthur Lane of Green Bay, Dave Hampton of Atlanta and Buffalo's Simpson, who was doing better than any of them at midseason.

It was long overdue, this return of the runner to prominence, for the broken-field run always has been and always will be more exciting than the long pass—not more effective, necessarily, but more exciting. Running-backs were featured in major profiles in *Sport* and *Sports Illustrated* magazines and the major newspapers, and *Life* and *Newsweek* magazines did spreads on "The Year of the Runner."

The great runners were quoted on the tricks of their trade. O.J. said, "I'm not a punishing runner. A guy like Csonka really gets beat up. But I never let a defender get a good shot at me. What ruins runners are those quick linemen and backers. With a big guy you give him a shoulder fake and he can't get back. But a smaller, quicker man—Nick Buoniconti of Miami is the best—is going so hard he's giving you only one place to run. . . . The game is won in the trenches. . . . Let me get past the line and one-on-one with a guy and, well, that's my game. . . . You got to work with what you got. . . . If the hole is there you can get in and slide. But if it's not there, there's not much you can do."

You do what you can do as quick as you can do it, almost by instinct. Years of running have built it into the brain, which operates as a computer. The situation develops, triggering a reaction. You don't have time to reason out your moves. "Thinking," concluded O.J., "is what gets you caught from behind."

He and his Bills faced a staggering second half. After a home game with undefeated Miami, the Bills faced four straight games on the road and five of their final six on foreign fields.

Miami was too much, but the battling Bills gave them a good game as the Dolphins continued their march to an unbeaten fourteen-game regular season.

A short touchdown pass by Shaw put the Bills ahead, 6–3, in the early going. Miami led only 10–6 after one period. And after a scoring runback of an interception, the Dolphins led only 16–13 at intermission. And only 23–16 after three periods. A final tally wrapped it up at 30–16, but the 46,206 fans in Buffalo's ancient arena felt they'd seen their side give it a good go.

Simpson carried only thirteen times so was limited to 45 yards, but caught three passes, too. Afterwards, he shrugged and said, "It's still a loss."

Beginning their long run on the road in mid-November, they were bombed in Shea Stadium, New York, by the Jets, 41–3. Simpson rushed twenty times for 89 yards, bettering the star Jet runners John Riggins, who got 64 yards, and Emerson Boozer, who got 54 yards, but it was still a loss, and a one-sided one. Here, the club had lost five straight and could have collapsed.

It did not. In Boston's new suburban stadium in Foxboro, Massachusetts, the Bills battled to a dramatic 27–24 triumph over the New England Patriots. Simpson rushed twenty-two times for 103 yards, and scored on a short sensational 13-yard scamper, but fumbled at the Buffalo 40 to set up a late Patriots' score that put the home side ahead 21–17 with time running out. When Mike Walker added a 36-yard field goal with less than two minutes to go, victory seemed out of the Bills' reach.

However, Linzy Cole returned the kickoff 51 yards to the New England 47 and four plays later Shaw passed from the 42 to Bob Chandler, who took the ball over his shoulder and stepped into the end zone to score. With the extra point, the game was tied, 24–24, with fifty-one seconds remaining. After the kickoff, New England went for the victory, but Maurice Tyler intercepted a Jim Plunkett pass at the Buffalo 35 and sprinted 27 yards to the Patriots' 38. John Leypoldt then kicked a 45-yard field goal with only five seconds left to win, 27–24.

The Bills bounced into the dressing room whooping and hollering.

In Cleveland, they went right at the Browns, who were bouncing back from a slow start and mounting a winning streak toward a play-off spot. Simpson ran 6 yards for 6 points and Leypoldt added an extra point and a field goal for a 10–0 first quarter lead. Cleveland came back however and slowly wore the undermanned Bills down for a 27–10 triumph.

Simpson not only caught a couple of passes for 25 yards, but ran twenty-seven times for 93 yards, to reach 1,008 yards for the season, becoming the first rusher on the circuit to top the 1000-yard mark for the campaign, with eleven games gone.

In Baltimore, the Colts keyed on his rushes and contained him to 26 yards on fourteen carries and though he caught six passes for 62 yards, the Bills bowed, 35–7. Simpson did score the Bills' lone touchdown, which ended a string of seventeen straight quarters Baltimore had blanked the Bills.

Time now was running out for the team to salvage something from the season. Even as their new 80,000-seat palace was rising in suburban Orchard Park, ten miles from town, the Bills returned home for their final game at the 36-year-old War Memorial Stadium. A crowd of 41,583 turned out for the historic moment. Detroit, driving desperately for a play-off berth, was the foe, heavily favored.

Simpson was sensational. He carried twenty-seven times for 116 yards against the lethal Lion line. He sparked drive after drive. After a scoreless first period, old pal Earl McCullouch caught a short pass from Greg Landry for the first score. But Shaw and Hill collaborated on a long touchdown pass to tie it, 7–7, before halftime. Buffalo threatened to score just before intermission, but Simpson fumbled the ball away at the Lion 2.

Shaw and Chandler collaborated on another long, scoring pass to put the Bills ahead in the third quarter, but Landry and Nick Eddy teamed up on one to tie it before the period ended. Late in the final period, Shaw put Buffalo ahead again on a short pass to Jan White. But Landry drove the Lions 73 yards, finished off with a 37-yard scoring pass to Ron Jessie, with just over two minutes left to tie it, 21–21.

It wasn't enough. The extra effort by Buffalo had tied the Lions at the final gun and eliminated them from play-off contention. Buffalo fans rushed onto the field to tear down the goalposts after this last game in this old arena. Pleased by their upset tie, the Bills still were disappointed that they had blown the late lead and the victory. Simpson took the blame because of his fumble at the end of the first half, but he had done a big job on the day.

In Washington, the Bills played their final game of the 1972 season against the powerful Redskins, champions of their conference. It was a tough contest, played on a miserably cold, windy Sunday afternoon in mid-December before more than 50,000 fans. Coming on, if too late, the Bills surprised the heavily favored foe.

Alvin Wyatt picked off a Billy Kilmer pass and streaked 49 yards to a touchdown and John Leypoldt kicked a 23-yard field goal to give the Bills a 10–0 lead after one period. Washington sliced its deficit to 10–7 before intermission and drove to a 17–10 lead in the third quarter. However, in the fourth quarter, Simpson, who had been slicing through the defenders for sizable gains, slid, cut, and sprinted 21 yards to the tying touchdown.

With two minutes left, from midfield, Kilmer threw and it bounced off receiver Herb Mul-Key's hands and into the hands of Buffalo linebacker Dale Farley, just off the taxi squad, and he lumbered 42 yards down the sidelines before Mul-Key hauled him down on the 3. Simpson hit into the line. Then he decoyed and big Jim Braxton hit in and carried the ball over for the winning score with forty-six seconds remaining.

The game ended 24–17, Buffalo in a big upset over Washington, and later Redskin coach George Allen said, "Losing is like death. Simpson killed us." O.J. had rushed twenty-six times for 101 yards, his sixth time of the season he had rushed for 100 or more yards, and he raised his total for the season to 1,251 yards on 292 carries, the best not only in his American Conference, but the best in the entire National Football League.

An injury to Larry Brown had sidelined him the last two games and left him with 1,216 yards, but Simpson had stayed ahead of the brilliant Redskin most of the season and simply pulled away at the finish.

No fewer than nine rushers gained 1,000 yards or more.

The two former Heisman Trophy winners from USC, Simpson and Garrett, were the only players with losing teams and inefficient blocking lines to top the 1000-yard mark. And Simpson, despite a line that was decimated by injuries all season, topped them all. He averaged more than 4 yards a carry; 4.3 to be exact. He had averaged 4.1 twice and 3.9 twice in his four prior years with the Bills, so the difference was simply that he got to carry the ball a reasonable number of times.

"I was happy when Lou Saban took over as our coach," Simpson said. "All I wanted was to carry the ball and I knew when he came here I would carry it."

"I kind of like winning the rushing title, but Larry Brown's a great runner and it took him not playing for me to get it," the modest Simpson noted.

However, Simpson actually carried the ball only seven more times than Brown's 285 and had a higher average per carry than Brown. The Giants' Ron Johnson carried the ball six more times than Simpson. Simpson did surpass the great Cookie Gilchrist's Buffalo records for most carries and most rushing yardage in a single season set when the Bills had a top team and blasting blocking in the line, and O.J. was in a position to take over the career team standards in 1973.

Shaw threw for more than 1,600 yards and with their late rush of upsets the Bills concluded the second half at 2–4–1 and the long season at 4–9–1, which enabled them to escape the cellar a game and a half ahead of New England, a mere half game behind Baltimore in the Eastern Division of the American Conference.

Simpson said, "We have a young team, but they keep hustling. Next year our guys will be healthy and who knows what can happen?" Coach Saban said, "When you consider all the problems we've had with our offensive line, it's remarkable to see that he got over a thousand yards. We lost seven offensive linemen this year and seldom had the same combination in there two games in a row. Simpson sparked us. He is a superstar. If we can surround him with a few more quality players we can improve and become competitive as a team."

O.J. Simpson not only was selected to the National Football League All-Star team and to the Pro Bowl roster, but he was a runaway winner of the voting to name the American Conference's Player of the Year, far in front of Franco Harris, Earl Morrall, and Larry Csonka. "Hey, it's a thrill," Simpson grinned. "O.J. feels as though he has arrived as a pro." He certainly had.

He ran 16 times for 112 yards and two touchdowns in the Pro Bowl, the best rushing record in the classic since it was converted to a clash of the two conferences; his American Conference nosed out the National Conference in a thriller, 33–28; and O.J. was a unanimous choice as Most Valuable Player in the game. "Hey," he said to the reporters who swarmed around him afterward, "this is just unreal."

He grew a Fu Manchu mustache, began a business with buddy Cowlings dealing with real estate and construction investments, and spoke of gaining 1,500 yards in 1973 during the off-season. This was a refreshed O.J. Simpson, who said, "I'm not talking of leaving after five years now. I wasted some years. It's all in front of me now." Confidently, he predicted, "My Buffalo team is gonna surprise some people."

He was right in every respect. Saban had shaped a strong team. Cowlings had been traded. Moses had been traded. Harris had gone to the Rams. But with big rookie Paul Seymour added to such young blockers as Reggie McKenzie and Donnie Green, even Jimmy Brown's 1963 pro football record of 1,863 yards rushing in a single season seemed not beyond O.J. and with a new quarterback Joe Ferguson easing in, a respectable record was not beyond the Bills Simpson now captained.

In the opener at Foxboro, Massachusetts, O.J. ran 80 yards on one carry and 250 yards on 29 carries and the Bills romped, 31–13. The regulars, including Simpson, were resting out the last part of the romp when someone told Saban O.J. needed 15 yards for a new one-game pro football rushing record. Fearful of injury, Saban warily put O.J. back in the game. He gained 15. Then someone said he still needed 15 more. Saban left Simpson in, and he gained 15 more. He had surpassed the 247-yard standard Willie Ellison had set two seasons earlier.

"I'm glad he got the record. He's a man, a great team man," Saban said.

Simpson smiled and said, "It's a great team. I don't think anyone will criticize this line. They've been telling me they're gonna get me some records. The way they block, I can't miss. The way they block, I don't even mind blocking for them."

At San Diego the second Sunday, the Bills suffered a letdown and lost, 34–7, but Simpson still gained 103 yards in 22 tries. The Bills bounced back in the official opener at their new Orchard Park suburban stadium, nipping New York's Jets, 9–7, before an enormous turnout of 80,020, and Simpson rolled 123 yards in 24 runs.

Philadelphia came to visit, more than 72,000 came to see, and the Bills pulled it out, 27–26, on John Leypoldt's late field goal as Simpson went 27 times for 171 yards.

Baltimore came to town, more than 78,000 came to

the game, and the Bills blasted, 31–13, with Simpson gaining 166 yards in 22 rushes. He went 78 yards on one, breaking five tackles on a spectacular scoring sprint.

By then the Bills had won four of their first five; Simpson had an incredible 813 yards in this short stretch; he was the hottest star in his sport, again a headlined hero; and his team seemed on its way to the top, if not this year, then in some year not very far away.

Then, on October 29 against the Kansas City Chiefs, O.J. rushed for 157 yards and became the first player in National Football League history to gain more than 1,000 yards in seven games. He scored two touchdowns, and the Bills won 23–14.

Overcoming obstacles that were enormous, struggling with a loser, settling himself in a faraway city, he was a mature man of twenty-six as he played his fifth professional season in 1973. The Player of the Year, the Player of the Decade from college competition had finally become the Player of the Year in pro play. O.J. Simpson faced a future filled with promise.

Finally, on December 16 against the New York Jets, some of that promise was realized when O.J. shattered Jim Brown's rushing record and became the first runner in National Football League history to gain over 2,000 yards in a season. In a game when the Bills defeated the Jets, 34–14, O.J. wound up the season with 2,003 yards rushed—well ahead of the 1,863 yards Brown amassed ten years previously.

Index

Abramoski, Eddie, 137
Alcindor, Lew, 61, 116
Aldridge, Rikki, 11, 12–13, 15, 47, 49, 54, 72
Allen, George, 121, 139, 184
Allmon, Dick, 14, 49, 81, 123
Alworth, Lance, 122
Anderson, Max, 136, 137
Andretti, Mario, 114
Andrusyshyn, Zeno, 10–12, 13, 71, 97
Arnett, Jon, 39, 40
Augustine, Don, 134
Ayala, Ron, 87, 88, 95, 101

Banks, Ernie, 22, 145
Barnes, Bruce, 168
Barnes, Chuck, 114–20, 126, 132, 133–34, 135, 146, 168, 171
Basilio, Carmen, 57
Bass, Dick, 40, 109
Battle, Mike, 46, 47, 49, 54, 81
Baugh, Sammy, 105
Beban, Gary, 8, 11–12, 13, 16, 61, 68, 70–72, 76, 78, 79
Bednarik, Chuck, 106
Biggs, Verlon, 149
Bleier, Rocky, 51, 54
Boozer, Emerson, 181
Bradley, Bill, 47
Bramlett, John, 150
Braxton, Jim, 175, 184
Briscoe, Marlin, 136, 148, 159, 160, 167
Brockington, John, 179
Brodie, John, 175
Brown, Bubba, 87
Brown, Jim, 26, 56–57, 58, 59, 108, 168, 186
Brown, Larry, 179, 184, 185
Brown, Willie, 132–33
Buffalo Bills, 112*ff*., 131–44, 137*ff*., 145*ff*., 157*ff*., 170*ff*.

Bulaich, Norm, 165
Buoniconti, Nick, 144, 180

Cameron, Paul, 40
Cannon, Jimmy, 112, 148
Cashman, Pat, 11, 71
Casper, Billy, 122
Cavanaugh, Ed, 172
Chandler, Bob, 81, 86, 176, 181, 183
Chapin, Dwight, 125, 126
Clark, Don, 43
Cole, Linzy, 181
Cowlings, Al, 24–25, 30, 81, 89, 157, 178, 186
Csonka, Larry, 165, 166, 179, 186
Cureton, Mickey, 97

Daimes, George, 68
Darragh, Dan, 143, 148, 158
Davenport, Bob, 40
Davis, Al, 48, 136
Day, Tom, 136, 137
Devaney, John, 155
Dickerson, Sam, 81, 99
DiMaggio, Joe, 23
Dooley, Jim, 172
Drake, Ron, 14
Drury, Morley, 39
Dubenion, Elbert, 137, 173
Durko, Mickey, 99
Durko, Sandy, 95
Durslag, Melvin, 56–57, 117

Eddy, Nick, 183
Ellison, Willie, 187
Elston, Dutch, 29–33, 62
Enyart, Bill, 94–95, 136, 137
Ewbank, Weeb, 141, 149, 159

Farley, Dale, 184
Farmer, George, 12, 71
Felser, Larry, 142, 144

INDEX

Ferguson, Joe, 186
Fertig, Craig, 132
Flores, Tom, 138
Foyt, A. J., 114
Franklin, Jim, 93

Galileo High School, 23*ff*.
Garrett, Mike, 33, 39, 67, 76, 79, 146, 150, 152, 179, 184
Gifford, Frank, 39
Gilchrist, Cookie, 136, 185
Gillman, Sid, 121, 123, 165
Gladieux, Bob, 99
Godfrey, Dr. Joseph, 161
Gonso, Harry, 73
Goux, Marv, 34, 44–45, 52, 71, 132, 154
Grady, Sandy, 14
Grady, Steve, 69
Grantham, Larry, 159
Green, Donnie, 164, 186
Griffin, Merv, 146
Gunn, Jim, 46, 81
Gustafson, Mark, 11

Hall, Charlie, 48
Hamilton, Tom, 96
Hampton, Dave, 179
Hanratty, Terry, 51, 52, 53, 54, 79
Hardy, Keven, 51, 53
Harmon, Tom, 40
Harris, Franco, 179, 186
Harris, Jim, 136, 137, 143, 157–58, 164, 165, 166, 173, 186
Hayes, Woody, 101, 103
Hayhoe, Bill, 12, 13, 71
Haywood, Spencer, 116
Hill, Cal, 168, 179
Hill, J. D., 167, 176, 182
Holmgren, Mike, 86
Horowitz, Steve, 87
Horrigan, Jack, 135, 146
Hubbard, Marv, 179

Indiana University, 72*ff*.
Isenbarger, John, 73

Jackson, Ruby, 30
Jarvis, Bruce, 164
Jessie, Ron, 183
Johnson, Harvey, 163–64, 166, 172
Johnson, Ron, 179, 185
Jones, Deacon, 139, 167
Jones, Greg, 10, 11, 70, 157
Jones, Parnelli, 114

Kaer, Mort, 98
Kelly, Leroy, 108, 121, 179
Kemp, George, 82
Kemp, Jack, 136, 141, 142, 143, 147–48, 150, 157
Keyes, Leroy, 78–79, 85, 98, 100, 105
Khasigian, Fred, 81
Kilmer, Bill, 40, 183–84
Klein, Bob, 46, 81, 93

Lamonica, Daryle, 143
Landry, Greg, 182–83
Lane, MacArthur, 179
Lawrence, Jim, 46, 47, 49, 64, 81, 86, 87, 93
Lee, Bob, 30
Lehmer, Steve, 14, 64
Levy, Dave, 66
Leypoldt, John, 181–82, 183, 187
Lindsay, Greg, 93
Little, Floyd, 142, 171, 174
Little, Lawson, 23
Lockton, David, 134
Lustig, Bob, 137, 173

Main, Billy, 95
Manke, Tom, 89
Matson, Ollie, 29, 31
Mays, Willie, 35–37
McBride, Jack, 22, 23, 24
McCoy, Mike, 100
McCullouch, Earl "The Pearl," 11, 31, 46, 50, 64–65, 66, 71, 111, 114, 182
McDole, Ron, 136
McElhenny, Hugh, 108–9
McFarland, Dave, 25
McInerney, Larry, 25–26
McKay, Corky, 44
McKay, John, 7*ff*., 29, 40, 41*ff*., 48, 49, 50, 51–52, 54, 55, 56, 58, 60, 66*ff*., 74, 83–84, 93*ff*., 123, 173
McKenzie, Reggie, 171, 173, 186
McMillan, Bo, 172
Michigan State University, 48–50
Minnesota University, 82–83
Mohler, Orv, 39, 86
Morris, Eugene "Mercury," 51, 179
Moses, Haven, 136, 137, 159, 186
Mul-Key, Herb, 184

Nagurski, Bronco, 105
Namath, Joe, 141, 159
Nobis, Tommy, 105, 106

INDEX

Notre Dame University, 51–54, 98 ff.
Northwestern University, 84
Nuttall, Dave, 12, 71

Oates, Bob, 15, 74
O'Donnell, Joe, 154
Ohio State University, 100 ff.
O'Leary, Tom, 53
O'Malley, Jack, 81, 87
Oregon State University, 68–69, 70, 94–95
Owens, Jim, 89, 90

Page, Toby, 11, 14, 46, 72
Parish, Don, 86, 88
Parker, Jim, 106
Parseghian, Ara, 55, 100
Patrick, Wayne, 136, 143
Plunkett, Jim, 86–87, 88, 89, 166, 181
Pont, John, 72, 74
Poppin, George, 23
Prothro, Tommy, 8ff., 43, 97

Ralston, John, 86, 88
Rauch, John, 113, 137, 140, 142, 144, 148, 154, 160, 162, 163
Ray, Johnny, 53
Reilly, John, 164
Riggins, John, 179, 181
Roberts, C. R., 39, 67
Robinson, Jack, 40
Rose Bowl game, 72–77, 97, 100–1
Rossovich, Tim, 46, 52
Royal, Darrell, 47–48
Rozelle, Pete, 134

Saban, Lou, 136, 142, 170–71, 172, 173–74, 175–76, 178, 185, 186, 187
Saimes, George, 136
San Francisco City College, 28 ff.
Sayers, Gale, 58, 59, 108, 110, 120–21
Scott, Dan, 51, 81, 88, 89, 95, 97
Schmidt, Joe, 113
Seymour, Paul, 186
Shaw, Billy, 136
Shaw, Dennis, 157, 158–59, 160, 162, 164–65, 166–67, 173, 175, 176, 180, 181, 182, 185
Shaw, Gerry, 81, 87
Shula, Don, 143
Simpson, Carmelita (sister), 18
Simpson, Eunice (mother), 18–19, 20, 76
Simpson, Jason (son), 155

Simpson, Jimmy (father), 18, 19, 20
Simpson, Leon (brother), 18
Simpson, Marguerite Whitley (wife), 38–39, 51, 69, 76, 127–28, 155, 160, 169
Simpson, Orenthel James "O.J.,"
  big games, 7–17, 64–77
  birth and childhood, 18–27
  junior college, 28–40
  marriage, 38–39
  at U.S.C., 41–55, 92–103, 104 ff.
  as a player, 56–63
  Heisman trophy, 78–91, 98, 105
  statistics, 100, 103, 104 ff.
  draft and personal management, 112–21
  life-style, 122–30
  and Buffalo Bills, 131–44
  rookie year, 137 ff., 145–56
  second season, 157–69
  superpro, 170–88
Simpson, Shirley (sister), 18
Smith, Larry, 167
Smith, Sid, 81
Snow, Jim, 46, 54, 81
Sogge, Steve, 46, 47, 49–50, 52, 53, 72, 73–74, 81, 82, 86–87, 89, 93, 94–95, 97, 99, 102
Spurrier, Steve, 175
Stanford University, 86 ff.
Staubach, Roger, 105
Strangeland, Jim, 34

Talliaferro, Mike, 173, 177
Tatum, Jack, 102, 103
Taylor, Mike, 14, 30, 64, 149
Texas Longhorns, 47–48
Theisman, Joe, 99
Turner, Jim, 159
Tyler, Maurice, 181

Unitas, John, 114, 139
University of California at Los Angeles (UCLA), 7–17, 40, 43, 55, 68 ff., 94, 97
University of Miami, 86
University of Southern California (USC), 33ff., 41 ff., 56 ff., 64 ff., 78 ff., 92 ff., 104 ff.
University of Washington, 64 ff., 89 ff.

Valdiserri, Roger, 55

Walker, Mike, 181
Ward, Rodger, 114

Warmath, Murry, 83
Washburn, Cotton, 39
Washington, Gene, 86
Washington, Kenny, 40
White, Jan, 177, 183
Wilkinson, Bud, 101
Wilson, Ralph, 116–18, 120, 134, 140, 163, 170–71

Wilson, Tommy, 40
Wyatt, Alvin, 183

Yary, Ron, 46, 64, 149
Young, Adrian, 46, 54
Young, Willie, 164

The Author

Bill Libby, the author of more than twenty books and many articles in *Sport* and other magazines, is a past winner of the U.S. National Magazine Sports Writer of the Year award. Among his recent popular sports biographies from Putnam's are *Willie Stargell: Baseball Slugger; Pete Rose: They Call Him Charlie Hustle; Johnny Bench: The Little General.* Mr. Libby lives in Westminster, California, with his wife, Sharon, and two daughters, Allyson and Laurie.